It's Hard for Me to Live with Me

A Memoir

Rex Chapman
with Seth Davis

Simon & Schuster

New York   London   Toronto   Sydney   New Delhi

1230 Avenue of the Americas
New York, NY 10020

First Simon & Schuster hardcover edition February 2024

SIMON & SCHUSTER and colophon are registered
trademarks of Simon & Schuster, LLC

Simon & Schuster: Celebrating 100 Years of Publishing in 2024

For information about special discounts for bulk purchases,
please contact Simon & Schuster Special Sales at
1-866-506-1949 or business@simonandschuster.com.

The Simon & Schuster Speakers Bureau can bring authors to
your live event. For more information or to book an event,
contact the Simon & Schuster Speakers Bureau at
1-866-248-3049 or visit our website at www.simonspeakers.com.

Interior design by Lewelin Polanco

Manufactured in the United States of America

1   3   5   7   9   10   8   6   4   2

Library of Congress Cataloging-in-Publication Data
has been applied for.

ISBN 978-1-9821-9777-3
ISBN 978-1-9821-9779-7 (ebook)

This book is dedicated to my four children—
Zeke, Caley, Tatum, and Tyson.
Thank you for the honor of being your dad.

It is also dedicated to anyone who has ever been addicted to
opioids. If I can overcome it, I promise you can, too.

Let everything happen to you:
Beauty and terror.
Just keep going.
No feeling is final.

—Rainer Maria Rilke

I hope to have God on my side,
but I must have Kentucky.

—Abraham Lincoln

Prologue

I climb into my car and drive through the gate outside my rented condo. In a flash, I am surrounded by four police cars. I slam on my brakes.

The cops rush to my door and bark at me to get out. They grab my arms, slam me against the hood, shove my wrists behind my back, cuff me, and stuff me into the backseat of a cruiser.

What the fuck, man?

It is Friday, September 14, 2014. I have no idea why this is happening. My initial thought is that it is because I have been driving with a suspended license—again. My license first expired in 2005. I never renewed it. Drove another six years without getting a new license. Got pulled over by the cops a few times. Sometimes they'd let me go, sometimes they'd give me a ticket, a couple of times they impounded my car. A few times I went to court to get the license back, but within a week I'd get another letter saying my license was suspended. Whatever. I just kept going. My mind is eroded from all the Suboxone. You're only supposed to be on it for a few months. I've been taking it for ten years. But four cars and handcuffs 'cause of a suspended license?

As I sit in the backseat trying to shake off the cobwebs, I ask the cops, "What am I being arrested for?"

One of them chuckles and says, "Oh, just a light day for crime in Scottsdale."

They drive me to the Maricopa County jail. I am worried because I am supposed to pick up my daughters at school. What will they think when I don't show up? How will they reach me? How will they get home?

The cops bring me inside the station and take all my personal belongings, including my wallet. That is a big problem because my medicine is in that wallet. I can't go more than a few hours without it. I hope they won't keep me long.

They press my fingerprints, snap my mug shot, and walk me down a hallway full of jail cells. They put me in a cell and shut the door behind me. *Clank.* There is another dude already in there. He is hunched in a corner, buck naked and trying to jack off.

After about fifteen minutes, one of the cops comes over. "Your phone's blowing up," he says. "Do you know any numbers by heart you can call?"

I only know one. My ex-wife, Bridget. She is about the last person I want to talk to at the moment.

He hands me the phone. It isn't easy to dial her number because I am getting bombarded with text messages. People are asking me if I'm okay. I'm like, how do they even know what's going on? I swallow my pride and call Bridget. She has heard the news, too, and asks what I want her to do. "Call Gus," I say, referring to a buddy of mine who I know will be able to get hold of an attorney.

Finally, a couple of detectives come and get me. They bring me into an interview room, sit me down, and start asking me some questions. One of the detectives asks, "Have you ever been to the Apple Store at the Scottsdale mall?"

Now I understand just how much trouble I am really in.

"I think I'd like to talk to a lawyer," I say.

End of interview.

They put me in a van and drive me to a station downtown. It has been about six hours since I have taken the medicine. I am starting to feel really sick. I try to tell the officers how badly I need it, but they have no interest in helping out.

The wagon pulls into a parking garage. I look out the window and see a bunch of TV camera crews waiting for me. "That's pretty fucked up," I say.

The female cop in the front seat replies, "Well, don't do fucked-up shit, and things won't be so fucked up."

They process me again, take my mug shot, and put me in a jail cell. It is nasty. There is peanut butter and all kinds of gross shit on the walls and all over the floor. I catch a glimpse of myself in a mirror hanging on the wall. It isn't a mirror, really, just one of those shiny, flat things you see in grade school.

But the reflection is clear enough. My face looks puffy. My eyes look cloudy. I notice I am wearing a Nike T-shirt with the words "Basketball Never Stops" printed on it. *Shit sure fucking stopped now, didn't it?*

After a long, sleepless night, I am taken at 6:00 a.m. to appear in front of a judge. Then they let me go. As soon as they hand me my wallet, I dig out that sheet of medicine and put it under my tongue. I have no way to get home, so I start walking toward the freeway, my mind in a total fog. It's hot, and after twenty minutes my son, Zeke, finds me and pulls up in his car. He gets out, comes around to hug me, and starts bawling. He keeps asking me over and over if I am okay. I know I'm sad, but I don't really feel it. I barely console him. That's what life is like when you're addicted to drugs. You just go numb. Here I am, worst moment of my life. Worst moment of his, too. Zeke is completely broken up, and yet I don't even shed a tear.

I climb into his car. After about five minutes, the medicine kicks in. I feel much better as Zeke drives me home. Out one prison, back into another.

It's Hard for Me to Live with Me

chapter

1

I wake up one morning when I am six years old, and I realize my mom and dad are gonna die. Maybe not that day, or even soon, but some day, eventually, they are gonna die. So am I. So is everyone around me. It makes everything seem pointless.

My parents get along okay, but they argue from time to time, like all married couples do. When they do, I have a terrible fear they will get divorced. Not just a fear, a certainty. It is gonna happen for sure.

I have a birthday party or play a basketball game or get some presents on Christmas, and I'll be happy for a while. When it is over, I'll start thinking, *Why even have a birthday party if we're all gonna die? What's the endgame here?*

I have a gift for imagining worst-case scenarios. If I am riding in a car and we see a man standing by the side of the road, I can picture the car hitting him. Same thing if I see a deer. One time my dad actually did crash into a deer. The thing came right through the windshield. It was terrifying but also validating. *See? Bad things are always gonna happen. I knew it!*

I don't feel like I can tell anyone what I am thinking, so I stay as busy as I possibly can. My poor mom. I wear that lady out, telling her a million times, "I'm *booooorrrred.*"

She'll sigh and say, "Rex, it's good to be bored sometimes." I look at her like she has two heads.

I sit in front of the TV for hours trying to keep my mind occupied. I love all the shows—*Perry Mason, The Honeymooners, The Jeffersons, Sanford and Son, Get Smart, Murder, She Wrote, The Brady Bunch.* But watching TV requires sitting still, which is a big-time problem for me. Before long, I'll be out the door and riding my bike all over the neighborhood, looking for games to play and generally being a pest to everyone I meet.

I am always getting hurt. One time I crash my bike, flip over the handlebars, and break my right wrist. Another time I break a finger running and jumping over stuff in a friend's basement. Another time I partially tear my Achilles tendon. They put me in a plaster walking cast and tell me to stay off it for six weeks. I bust through three of those casts. My dad catches me a few times running around on it in the gym and cusses me out. I tell him I'm sorry, but I don't really mean it. The best way to get out of my head is to keep my feet moving.

● ○ ●

Dad's job as a basketball coach has us moving around a lot. He played basketball in college and in the old ABA. We lived in an apartment in Bowling Green, Kentucky, when I was a baby, and then moved to Owensboro when I was three. After a year in kindergarten, we moved again. My parents had started me in school a year too early, I assume because they wanted me out of the house, but now they have me repeat kindergarten so I can be back with kids my own age. They are already thinking I might be an athlete, so they figure that's what's best for my future. Still, it's a little embarrassing to have to attend kindergarten again. My dad tells me, "If anyone asks why you're going to kindergarten again, tell them you've been redshirted."

One of my mom's best friends who lives across the street has a son named Billy Joe Burton. He is a year ahead of me in grade school and was born with severe physical deformities. His wrists and ankles are completely turned in. Mom asks me to walk with him to school every day. Billy Joe moves very slowly. He had a bunch of surgeries and has to wear big braces on his legs. There are a couple of times he falls down and has a seizure, and that freaks me out. It takes a while for us to get to school, but I don't care. I think Billy Joe is hilarious.

I feel a responsibility for Billy Joe, and I also feel guilty because my legs work just fine—better than fine, actually. The toughest part is seeing other kids tease him at school. Lunch is the worst. I try to stick up for him as best I can.

At the end of my third-grade year, Dad decides to quit coaching and takes a public sector job in Frankfort. Switching schools isn't easy for a shy, awkward kid like me. I am self-conscious about my gigantic gums and the gap between my front teeth. I have a big cowlick on the right side of my head that is impossible to fix. If I don't know you, I'm not gonna try to talk to you—that is, until I get to PE class. Then I really step out.

When I get into a competitive situation, my personality changes completely. Man, do I like to win. Scratch that—I hate to lose. Fucking *hate* it. In PE, I am out for blood. If I know we are gonna play kickball, I wear two different sneakers, because I believe that I can kick the ball farther with the shoe on my right foot. I tie my laces with bunny ears because I don't know how to tie them right. It is a skill I will never master.

And don't *even* let it be Bombardment Day. That's what we call dodgeball. They actually hand me these bouncy orange balls and tell me to throw them at my classmates as hard as I can. Like, that is the *requirement* of that class. Are you shitting me?

I love it when the other kids try to get me out, because it is so easy for me to catch the balls. The teacher keeps saying we aren't supposed to aim at people's heads, but well, you know, accidents happen sometimes. One day I accidentally take out a girl. I feel bad about it, but the teacher finally has enough. He jumps in with the other team and starts firing. He fakes at me and I fall for it. When I jump in the air, he throws and hits my feet so hard, they flip up in the air and I land on my head. The game stops. I lie on the ground with the wind knocked out of me, trying not to cry. The teacher, Tim Taylor, who is also my first basketball coach, comes over to me and expresses all kinds of concern, but I can tell by the smirk on his face that he isn't the least bit sorry.

I am competitive about everything. One time my buddies and I are having a little competition at the urinals in the boys' bathroom. There are no barriers between the urinals, so we decide to see who can "jump" the urinals with their pee. Evel Knievel is our inspiration, because he just jumped the Grand Canyon with his motorcycle. I am intent on winning. Which I do—except I pee so far it lands right on another kid, who runs out of the bathroom screaming. I get sent to the office, where the principal proceeds to give me a couple of licks with a paddle.

Swimming is my main sport at first. I am so fast that they move me up to race against older kids. I am six years old and beating nine- and ten-year-olds in the breaststroke pretty easily. I love it until some of the older girls start calling me Sexy Rexy. When I complain to my mom, she laughs. "That's a compliment, Rex," she says. Sure doesn't feel like one.

Eventually I get self-conscious about having to wear those little Speedo racing suits. It wouldn't be so bad except we practice at a public outdoor pool next to a baseball field. My buddies ride by on their bikes headed for baseball practice and make fun of the way I look in that Speedo. So much for swimming.

I try baseball next. I can't hit because I am afraid of the ball. I am a really good shortstop and also pitch some. I can throw hard, but I am real wild. Strikeouts and walks are my deal.

One time I am pitching in this big game, and a guy hits a comebacker right at me. I field it cleanly but throw it over the first baseman's head. Our right fielder isn't paying attention, so I have to chase the ball down myself while a run scores. I try to throw the runner out at third, but once again, it sails too high. He scores, we lose. I go home, shut myself in my room, and curse my teammates, even though it's my fault we lost.

So much for baseball.

I play some football, too. The first time I try to play, I'm too light, but the next season my dad stuffs my pockets with coins so I can meet the weight minimum. I make two great friends in Keith and Kevin Vanderpool, twin brothers who live in the neighborhood, but I don't like the sport at all. After a week of practice, I tell my folks I want to quit. They resist. Finally, my dad says, "Here's the deal. You have one 'quit' and you can use it whenever you want. If you use it now, you can't ever quit anything else you decide to do." That's an easy choice for me. I am done with football.

It is inevitable that I would decide to be a basketball player. Not only am I living in Kentucky, a state that loves the sport more than just about anything, but I've been around my dad's teams since I could walk. I was a good dribbler before most of my friends even picked up a ball. If I play basketball against the kids in grade school who are my own age, it is like going up against babies. When I was in first grade, they had this stupid rule that said you couldn't defend full court. So I'd wait impatiently at the half-court line. I know that no one can dribble with their off hand, so all I have to do is sit on the strong hand, take the ball from the guy when he tries to switch, and race in for an easy layup. Eventually they made that against the rules, too. When my parents have friends or relatives over, Mom or Dad will say, "Have you seen Rex play?" They show up to my next game, and I just know they are expecting me to get 40. So I give 'em what they want. It is easy, and it gives me a sense of self-worth that I can't get anywhere else.

I play my first real big game when I am in Tamarack Elementary School. We have a PE basketball tournament, and my team makes the finals. I am in fourth grade, but I am by far the best player in the school. By the time the game starts, the gym is packed. I come out for warm-ups, look into the stands, and see that not only is my dad there, but all of the players on his high school team are there as well. Those guys are my heroes.

As I walk to midcourt for the opening tip, the enormity of the moment overcomes me, so I do what comes naturally.

I puke.

I'm not talkin' about itty-bitty spit-up here. I mean, I fucking hurl my entire breakfast right there on the midcourt circle. They have to delay the start of the game so someone can bring out a big mop and clean it all up. I am really embarrassed, but I also feel a lot better. There is never a doubt I am gonna play. They start the game, and I dominate like always while leading my team to the championship.

From that point on, I am a regular puker. This is another thing I get from my dad. I'll be in his locker room before games, listening to him give his pregame pep talk, and then he'll go into a bathroom stall to vomit. Most of the time it is dry heaves. That's how nervous he gets. By the time I am in middle school, I am throwing up before almost every game. Over time, I try not to eat too much on game days, but I will still head into that bathroom and stick my finger down my throat. I do it all the way through to my first few years in the NBA, but after a while I have to stop. Those are eighty-two-game seasons. You can't be barfing before every game. But if I didn't do it and I played shitty, a teammate or a trainer would turn to me and say, "It's because you didn't throw up."

● ○ ●

My dad is a local legend from his playing days at Western Kentucky and the pros, but I am too young to realize that. All I know is I want to be like him. Dad is a really good coach, but from the time I start playing, he is adamant about not coaching my teams. There is only one time he does. It is during the brief period when he isn't coaching because he thinks he wants to try a normal job. I am in fourth grade, and my regular coach is out of town. He asks my dad to fill in for a practice and a game.

Before practice, Dad warns me, "I'm gonna be harder on you than on anybody else." He isn't lying. That man is on my ass from start to finish, but when the game comes around, he lets me do my thing. We win, of course. He never coaches me again.

Dad is pretty much out of the Bobby Knight school. His players get all his love and all his hate. They're afraid of him, but they love playing for him. There is an intimacy to that relationship, and I want to feel that with him, too. But Dad never takes me out on the court. Not once. Never says, "Let's go shoot around," never plays one-on-one, never offers to work me out, never even rebounds for me. He's not ignoring me, he just wants me to come to the game on my own. I've seen enough dads around town get so involved with their kids, coaching them hard and thinking they're gonna be big-time players when I know they're not. Part of me likes that my dad leaves me alone. If I do something well, I can see the look on his face that shows he's impressed.

Even so, I love being around Dad's teams. As soon as school is out, I head over to practice. I sit in the bleachers, get my homework done as fast as I can, and grab a ball. The only rule is I can't bounce it when he is talking. I stand in the corner, watch those guys intently, and imitate their every move. I dribble behind my back and between my legs without realizing it is supposed to be hard. He even lets me hang out in the locker room during games. Many times he comes in at halftime and he is so raging mad, he goes up to each player, gets in his face, and goes right on down the line saying, "Chickenshit . . . Chickenshit . . . Chickenshit . . ." He is a beautiful cusser.

If his team loses, the next morning things will be real tense in our house. I'll come into the kitchen, and Mom will be serving him microwave bacon. He drinks Coke from a bottle and smokes a cigarette in silence. My sister and I know not to make too much noise or say anything to him for a few days. If he gets real mad, my mom tries to play the peacemaker. She chooses her spots, but if she tells him to stay quiet and he is being an ass, he will, in his own way, let her know she is right.

Our fifth-grade team is undefeated for a while. We finally lose a game and I show my frustration. My dad pulls me aside and says, "Rex, you can't show up your teammates. Some of 'em can't catch those passes. So you should take the blame when they drop 'em. That takes the heat off them." It is a really good lesson that I never forget. From that point on, I make it a point to love up my teammates all through my career.

The season ends in a double-elimination tournament. On the day of the finals, I jack up a ton of shots and we lose real bad. I am inconsolable. I go home and I crash in my room. We have to play the second game that night. To me, it is as big as the seventh game of the World Series. Once I calm down a little, my dad comes into my room and says, "You know all those twenty-footers you took? Those could all be layups. You can get by these guys any time you want." I trust that advice, and when the second game starts, I slice right through everybody. Must've scored 50 just shooting layups.

After being out of basketball for a year, Dad can't stand it anymore. He takes a job as the head coach at Hancock County High School in Lewisport. That puts us closer to Owensboro, which means I can spend lots of time again playing at the Dugan Best Center. That's where all the Black kids in town play. Dad has a lot of Black friends from his playing days, so they connect me with their kids. I was in first or second grade the first time Dad dropped me off there, back when we first lived in Owensboro.

I start spending lots of time on the outdoor court on Fifth Street in the heart of Owensboro's Black neighborhood. Most of the players are a couple of years older than me, and they are really good. That is the first time I go up against guys who are better, and it drives me crazy. Some days I feel like I don't play well, and I spend all night thinking about some dude who busted my ass. I can't wait to go back the next day and get him back. I can't take not being good enough.

My parents really walk the walk when it comes to race. We'll be at a cocktail party or some type of gathering with white and Black people. When the Black people leave, someone will tell a racial joke. My mom and dad will look at each other and say, "Time to leave."

I hear that a new network called Black Entertainment Television is starting up. My mom asks me, "Why do you think there's no such network as White Entertainment Television?"

I think for a second and reply, "Don't we already have white entertainment all over the place?"

"Exactly."

Through those games at Fifth Street and other mostly Black areas of town, I make friends a lot more easily than I ever do in school. They live a lot differently than I do. I go to their houses and see that there are seven or eight people living in a small one-bedroom apartment. Some of the apartments don't have heat or AC, and the people who live there might not eat three meals a day. My family is far from rich. We don't have a ton of dough, and we rent houses instead of own them. But I always have my own room, we always have air-conditioning, and there is always food in the fridge. Seeing how my friends live makes me feel grateful, and more than a little guilty. It isn't fair.

● ○ ●

My dad is tough on us. He doesn't spank us often, but when he does, I figure out real quick that if I cry *before* he starts spanking me, it will be over more quickly. My sister, Jenny, is nearly two years younger than me, but she is tougher and a lot more stubborn. Bent over his lap, she takes her punishment in stoic silence. I think, *Just cry, goddammit, and it will be over.* When I was about seven years old, I got mad at Jenny for something and chased her around the house. I tried to kick her and missed, and I put my foot through a wall. Later that night, my dad came home from a road trip. He walked in around three in the morning, saw the hole, came into my room, and spanked me a couple of times. If Mom gets real mad at me, all she has to say is "You want me to tell your dad about this?" That's usually enough for me to change my behavior.

My dad grew up afraid of his own father, a man with a sixth-grade education who owned a restaurant and motel a few miles outside of Owensboro. If my dad stepped out of line, he got the business end of a switch or a belt. My grandfather died when my dad was twenty, so he didn't have anyone to show him how to be a dad. As a result, my dad formed a very old-fashioned view of gender roles. Many years later, when I have kids of my own, I'll ask my dad if he changed diapers when my sister and I were babies. "Nah," he'll say. "I went to change you once and you peed all over me. I told your mom, 'No more.'"

Mom was a cheerleader at Western Kentucky, where she met my dad. She got pregnant with me, married my dad, and left school after her sophomore year. They kept that chronology secret from me and my sister for a long time. All my friends love being around my mom, but they're terrified of my dad, who's really big and seems kind of mean. So most of the time when I have sleepovers it's at my friends' houses. She is honest, smart, funny, and sweet. Everyone loves my mom. She's like Lucille Ball. She has that kind of personality. Every morning, whether it is hot or cold, rainy or sunny, she goes out to the driveway in her robe, pretends to try to lift up the garage door and grunts real loud like it is hard work. She'll slip and fall on purpose to get a laugh out of us. She tells dirty jokes and is a great storyteller. All of that comes from being in a showbiz family. Her brother plays the bass and sings in a band, and their mom was a well-known piano player who played in bars for about thirty years. She couldn't read music, but she could play anything you asked her to.

We spend a lot of time with my mom's family. She has a brother, Rex, who's only eight years older than me. He's one of my heros. I always look forward to her family coming over because they are funny. A lot of them are big drinkers. I'm too young to realize just how much addiction and mental illness there is in my family.

My parents don't argue a lot. When they do, it is usually over my dad going to the racetrack. I was about six years old when he started taking me along. I learned how to read a racing form before I was really reading in school.

I love when I come home from school and he says, "You want to go to Ellis Park?" He gives me twenty bucks. The rule is, I can only place show bets, two bucks a race, and the rest covers my hot dogs and sodas. I listen to him chat up his buddies. He looks over my shoulder while I handicap the race. He teaches me that if you play certain combinations and hedge your bets just right, you can almost buy a race. It is a foolproof system. Or so I think.

If he takes me to the track, it is under the condition that I am not, under any circumstances, allowed to tell my mom where we have been. This makes our adventures seem even more exciting. If she suspects us, she never lets on. We almost get caught on the day Elvis Presley dies. We hear the news on the radio while we are driving home from Ellis Park. We aren't supposed to be in a car long enough to be listening to a radio, so my dad tells me that when we get home, we have to pretend we don't know.

Having been raised in a big musical family, my mom is a huge Elvis fan. We walk in the house, and she is sitting in the kitchen just bawling. When my dad asks her what is wrong, she replies, "Elvis died."

"Wow, that's awful," I say, and hurry up to my room.

chapter

2

I don't watch a lot of NBA games because there are only one or two on TV per week. Most of the basketball that is on locally are college games. I learn a lot by watching those with my dad.

I'm still in middle school, but I'm allowed to play with the freshman team at Hancock High. So is my best friend, Mike Ogle. One time we are playing across the river in Cannelton, Indiana. The gym is located inside a fire station and it's real tight. The wall is just a couple feet behind the baseline. I chase a kid down on a fast break and time my block perfectly. I spike it out of bounds, volleyball-style, but it bounces off that wall right into the kid's hands. It happens so fast the ref doesn't see it, and when the kid makes a layup, they count the bucket. I go right up to the ref and shout, "Are you fucking kidding me?"

Everybody hears me. He tees me up. My mom can cuss the refs out as hard as anyone, but she doesn't like when I do it. "Wait until your dad gets home," she says when we get in the car.

On game days, I'm real anxious all day long. I know the only way we are gonna win is if I play well. This is Kentucky, remember. There are no meaningless basketball games. Even if there is a small crowd in a nothing middle school gym, the parents are screaming and cussing at the refs. Before the game starts, I go into the bathroom and stick my finger down my throat. Sometimes I heave so violently I burst blood vessels in my eyes. I've learned not to eat too much beforehand so the heaves will be a little gentler. Once I am done, I feel like Superman. Let's fucking go.

Most of my middle school games are a joke. I find better competition when I join an AAU team the summer before ninth grade. I am the only kid on the team who can consistently make shots from beyond fifteen feet, so I earn the nickname Radar. Eventually it gets shortened to Dar.

I am also the only white kid on the team. My teammates are the same guys I've been playing with and against around town for years. Avery Taylor, whose dad, Charlie, is one of my dad's best friends, is on the team, too. After one of our tournament games, someone makes a comment at dinner about us being a dark horse team. Charlie cracks, "Yeah, we're the dark horse riding the white horse." Everyone laughs, and I do, too, but something about that joke throws me off a little. Part of it is because we have other kids, like Avery, Marcus Robinson, and David "Pookie" Hogg, who as far as I'm concerned are just as good as I am, maybe even better. I don't see myself as this team's white horse, but apparently others do.

Our team travels around the state and crushes the competition. The coaches want to take us to a tournament in Memphis, so we wash cars and do menial work on the weekends to raise money. We get to Memphis and win the championship, but we also trash our rooms. We spend the rest of the summer raising more money to pay for the damages.

Later that summer, we travel to South Bend, Indiana, for a big national tournament. We romp our way to the semifinals, where we get knocked off by a team that includes Brian Oliver, who will go on to play in a Final Four with Georgia Tech. Brian is fifteen, but he looks to me like he is twenty. We win the consolation game and take home the third-place trophy. It sucks not to win, but it proves that we can go anywhere, play anyone, and more than hold our own.

The biggest local event of the summer is the annual Dust Bowl Tournament in Owensboro. It takes place on Fifth Street, so you always see Black people and white people playing together and against each other. It's a great event, and as usual, my team dominates, so they move us up a couple of age groups. We keep right on winning until they finally have to put us in the men's division. Those guys beat the shit out of us and love doing it.

But beyond the basketball, the Dust Bowl is a great event

where you see people from all races, backgrounds, and economic levels come together to hang out, listen to music, eat food, and play basketball. It is what you would hope the world could be.

● ○ ●

The only time I get in trouble in middle school is when a really good friend of mine gets caught with pot in his locker. They bring us both into the principal's office. When the principal asks my buddy why he had the weed, he shrugs and says in his southern drawl, "It just makes life a little more tolerable." I have to bite my lip to keep from laughing.

I am also developing a sensitive streak, especially when it comes to vulnerable people who are not being treated well. I notice one day that there is a bully who keeps picking on a kid during lunch. Having just started at the school, I don't know anyone, but he does it for several days in a row, and it really bothers me. Finally, I come around the table, grab the guy by the head, and smash his face into his food. I get so mad while I'm fighting him, it's almost as if I black out. A couple of teachers pull me off him and send both of us to the main office. If my parents ever hear about the incident, they don't say anything to me.

● ○ ●

After two years coaching at Hancock County High, Dad moves on to an assistant's position at Kentucky Wesleyan, a

Division II college in Owensboro. I am glad because it means moving back to where I have a bunch of friends.

Like most high schools, Apollo has three levels—freshman, junior varsity, and varsity. I am only a freshman, but a couple of my buddies, Jeff Sanford and Greg Baughn, are gonna play varsity, so that is my hope as well. Problem is, in order to make varsity you have to run an eight-minute mile. I am only five foot seven and super skinny. I have big feet and am all legs. Greg lives across the street, so we wake up early every morning and go running. It feels like I am carrying cement on my shoulders.

On the day of the tryout, I run my best time ever, but I still miss the maximum by about fifteen seconds. I should be cut from the team, except the best player that year is a senior named Greg McFarland, and he was adamant that he wasn't gonna run the mile. The coach said he had to, so he walked it. No way the coach is gonna keep Greg off the team, so I guess he can't keep me off, either.

I am so excited when they give us our uniforms. That is the first year that players are allowed to have numbers under 10. I am given the number 3 and will wear it the rest of my career.

I am surprised to make varsity because of how small I am. I'm not even in puberty yet. When the team goes to the showers, I try to wait as long as possible until everyone is out of there because I am the only one in the locker room who doesn't have hair on his dick. Once we are on the court, I hold my own, but I also feel anxious about having to prove myself.

There is some chatter that the only reason I got put on varsity is because of my dad, but it doesn't take long to prove that I belong.

I also play every freshman and JV game that year. The JV game is usually right before the varsity game, so sometimes I am triple-dipping. I start off the season as the sixth man on varsity, but I get better as the season goes on. Eventually they tell me not to play JV games if they are on the same day as varsity.

Practices are tough. I am always anxious about playing well enough, and there are a couple of older guys who love to fuck me up because they don't like that I am stealing their minutes. I don't always like it, but I know it is good for me.

Still, I'm not satisfied. I complain to my dad that the coach isn't playing me enough, and he doesn't know what he's doing. He is not having it. "You don't think that coach wants to win?" he says. "If you want more minutes, you gotta play better." From that point on, I know for sure that if I ever want to talk shit about a coach, I will not have an ally in my father.

The varsity isn't very good, but we finish the season strong by beating Owensboro Catholic in the district play-offs. To my surprise, that summer I get invited to a basketball camp at the University of Kansas. My dad is buddies with the coach there, Larry Brown. The two best players at the camp in my grade are Kevin Pritchard and Steve Henson. They aren't much taller than me, but they are stronger, and they really know how to play. They also really want to kick my ass, and that's exactly what they do.

One thing about Pritchard that gets to me is the way he dunks. I have never been able to dunk, and seeing him do it so easily nags at me. By the end of the camp, I will my way into doing it. When I get home, I tell my buddies that I can dunk now, but they think I am full of shit. "Let's go right now and I'll show you," I say. We break through the window of the gym at Owensboro Middle School. I take a few dribbles, take off and dunk.

● ○ ●

We aren't a real religious family. I don't even know what my parents consider themselves. Baptists, I guess. They take us to church once in a while on Christmas and Easter and other special occasions. I'll sit there listening to all the stories the ministers say happened in the Bible and think, *Nope, bullshit, not true.* There is nothing about the whole story that resonates with me.

My mom does everything she can to get me to read, but that doesn't jibe with my limited attention span. She is a stickler for grammar. If I ever use the word *ain't*, she corrects me by saying, "Ain't ain't a word." One day she gets real excited because she buys us a set of encyclopedias with green covers on them. "Isn't this amazing?" she says, beaming. "Everything you could possibly need to know in the world is right here." *Really, Mom? Everything?*

Basketball comes easy to me. School is easy, too, until I get to algebra. It's the letters that throw me. I refuse to buy into the idea that they represent numbers. This becomes an even bigger problem in chemistry. My teacher is Miss Stamper, and I raise my hand and act like a jackass just to get through her class. It is fifty minutes of torture. When I ask one particularly annoying question, she looks at me exasperated and says, "Rex, this is just common sense." I flip out. She sends me to the principal. The next day, my parents come in for a meeting, and I get moved to another chemistry class.

I for sure know I'm not dumb. I just have this other thing going on that is far more worth my time and concentration. Yeah, some of my buddies get better grades than I do, but they study all the time. That doesn't seem very fun. I work one-tenth as hard as they do, and my grades are almost as good.

If I have a big term paper, someone else writes it for me, usually a girl. If I don't study for a test, I learn to cheat. One of my favorite English teachers, Mrs. Fortune, catches on to my little game. She tells me that for the next day's test on the book *Great Expectations*, I am gonna sit right next to her so she can be certain I don't copy anyone's paper.

I go home that night and read the whole thing. Come back the next day and get an A. Mrs. Fortune is convinced I cheated somehow. I tell her, "Go ahead and ask me whatever you want." I finally convince her.

I'm at least partially dyslexic, although I haven't been officially diagnosed and have no idea what that is. I'll take a test in school or write a paper and think I did really well, only to get it back and see that I missed some questions where I knew the answer but had made careless mistakes. I actually lose a basketball game once because I read the scoreboard wrong. When I grow up, I'll still have a hard time following directions in hallways and hotels. I'll step off an elevator, see the numbers on the wall with arrows indicating which way to go, and get lost. When I travel to road games as an NBA player, I learn to follow my teammates around the hotel hallways, hoping my room is near theirs.

Eventually, I'll be diagnosed with attention deficit disorder. People with ADD have a hard time locking in on things, but if they are really, really interested in something, they tend to hyperfocus. That's the case with me and basketball. If I am playing a game and shoot 0 for 12 in the first three quarters, it doesn't bother me, because I know that when it comes to crunch time, I am gonna lock in and make my shots. Basketball is just more interesting than algebra.

● ○ ●

I want more than anything in the world to be good at basketball. My dad is tall and everyone says a spurt is coming. I measure myself every single day on my bedroom door, hoping to catch even a bit of progress. That summer, away for a couple of weeks at the Kansas camp, I can't do my daily height check. The first thing I do when I get back is measure myself on that door.

It shows I am a full inch taller than the last marking. *That can't be right.* Pretty soon, I am dunking with regularity. My body is changing fast. Too fast. It isn't long before I start to experience really bad knee and back pain. I complain to my mom that my shoes are too small, but she swears they are the right size. They were—at the time we bought 'em.

I grow so fast, I get stretch marks on my back. My skin can't keep up with what my bones are doing. I wake up in the middle of the night and feel like my side is on fire. I have so much back pain, my mom takes me to a couple of doctors. They fit me for a back brace with a steel rod, and I have to wear it when I play.

By the time basketball season begins my sophomore season, I am six feet two, a good five inches taller than the year before. My reach has gotten real long, too. Basketball is all about length—you block shots with your hands, not your head—so that makes me even more dangerous as a player. I am still the youngest guy on the varsity, but I average about 20 points a game and jump center. Never lose a jump ball, not one time. I also play on the front line of our 1-3-1 zone because my arms are long and I am a good on-ball defender, and on the back of our 2-3 zone because I am the best re-bounder and shot blocker.

The pain gets so bad at times that I miss about five games. I do whatever I can to be on that court. My dad finds a chiropractor in town who adjusts me and then shoots me up with cortisone and Novocain. I'm pretty sure that vio-lates the whole do-no-harm oath that doctors are supposed to take, but I am desperate to play. It's the only thing I want to do in life.

Early in my sophomore year, I get my first recruiting

letter. It is from Illinois State. I am so excited, in my mind that's where I am going. I am just glad to know my parents won't have to pay for college. I notice Dad is starting to recruit some of the older high school players in the area to Kentucky Wesleyan, but he never tries to recruit me. It bugs me. When I ask why he is ignoring me, he seems surprised. "You may be too good to play for Kentucky Wesleyan," he says. Whenever I had a bad game, or a game where he thought I wasn't trying hard enough, he'd say to me, "You couldn't fuckin' play for me at Wesleyan." Him saying I'm too good to play there just about turns my world upside down. I had no idea he thought I was that good.

Word travels fast in Kentucky when it comes to basketball. Before long, our games are packed. The gym at the high school is too small, so we play downtown at Owensboro Sportscenter. The place holds more than five thousand fans, and most of our games are standing room only. Whatever shyness or social awkwardness I have completely disappears when those games begin. I love playing in front of those crowds, and I especially love going on the road to smaller gyms and seeing the place packed as well. I just know when I go out on that floor that I am gonna be way better than everyone. I know that there is nobody who works harder than I do or knows more about the game. I'll walk out onto the court, look around at all the fans, and think, *I'm so glad y'all are here to see what I'm about to do.*

Our games are covered pretty extensively in the local newspaper, and my picture is published after almost every game. I start to notice that people I don't know look at me funny. This is my first taste of celebrity. One day I go to the mall with my buddies. We pass a group of students who are from Daviess County High School, which is our cross-county rival. We are standing around eyeing each other when a few of the kids come over to me. A girl holds out a paper and pen and says, "Can you sign this?"

I don't know how to react. My buddies are watching and snickering as I sign. Then the girl turns around, goes back to her crew, and makes a big show of ripping it up. They think it is hilarious, and my friends do, too.

Funny how once I become known as a great basketball player, girls start to become more interested in me. I go to a New Year's Eve party midway through my sophomore year and start talking to this older girl. She has been out of high school for a year. At the end of the night, I go home. My parents are still out doing whatever they are doing for New Year's. Five minutes later there is a knock at the door. It is the girl from the party. We start fooling around and I take her up to my bedroom. All of a sudden, she pulls down my pants, climbs on top of me, and puts my dick right inside her. I panic. I don't have any birth control, and I have heard so many horror stories about how easily girls can get pregnant. I let her ride me for a few seconds, then push her off me and say, "I'm sorry. I can't." She is cool about it and leaves the house a short while later. It's a hell of a way to lose my virginity.

chapter

3

Greg and I get invited to a bunch of all-star camps the summer after my sophomore season. We turn down most of them so we can play in team camps around Kentucky. My reputation is really growing. I have a lot of natural ability, but the reason I am good is because I work at basketball. *Work* isn't even the right word. I am obsessed.

When I'm not at a camp or playing in a tournament, I am pedaling my bike with a basketball under my arm, looking for the best runs in town. I know that on Tuesdays at 4:00 p.m., Fifth Street is the place to be. The last game of the night usually happens at Chautauqua Park. Or I head over to Legion Park. Even after I get old enough to drive, I still ride my bike because I know it will make my legs strong. Sometimes I show up to these parks alone, but often I have a few teammates with me, especially Greg. He is quick and smart, and he is one tough motherfucker. He is always ready to fight anyone.

That includes me. Greg and I are around each other so much and both so competitive, it is inevitable we will square off from time to time. Our worst fight happens late one night at Legion Park. Everyone is gone, but we stay to play one-on-one as usual. We start arguing, one of us throws the ball at the other, and pretty soon the fists start flying. We stop after a while because we are exhausted.

The problem is that Greg is my ride, and I really don't want to walk home. We climb into his pickup truck and slam our doors hard. We don't say a word the whole way. Greg pulls into his driveway, which is right across the street from mine, and I get out and go into mine. The next morning, just like always, Greg rolls up and drives us both to school. We go about our day like nothing had happened.

Once the season starts, our team never plays in a gym that isn't completely full. One game early in the first quarter, I shoot a turnaround jump shot on the baseline, and one of the opposing players blatantly undercuts me. It is a real dirty play. The next time down the court, I bait the guy into guarding me on the same type of shot. He tries to box me out again before I land, only this time I yank him on my way down. We crumple to the floor as everyone, including the referees, run upcourt.

As I get up, I swing my left elbow and catch him flush on the nose. It breaks immediately. I mean, it explodes. There is blood everywhere.

The refs never saw what happened, but the opposing team's fans sure did. So did some of their players on the bench. One of them runs toward me and tries to tackle me, but Greg intercepts him. We finish the game, but the kid has to go to the hospital and comes back toward the end. He sits on the bench with a huge bandage on his face. Some of our fans traveled to the game. They serenade him with "Rudolph the Red-Nosed Reindeer."

The next morning, I am asked to meet with the principal, the athletic director, and our coaches. They tell me I can't do things like that, and I argue, "Did you see what he did to me?" They make me call the other team's coach and apologize, but they don't suspend me or anything like that. I am very lucky it wasn't on video. If more people had seen what happened, it most likely would have kept me from playing in college. It was that bad.

Our rivalry with Owensboro High goes to another level that season. We aren't just the two best teams in the city. We are the best in the state. We are all white, and they are all Black, but I am good friends with all of their players. Both teams' number one goal is to win the state tournament. You do that in Kentucky, you're immortal. Apollo has only been there one time, in 1978, when my dad was the coach. Greg and I are determined to get us there again.

As good as I am, the other teams are scared of two guys on our team, not one. Greg goes up against these teams who try to press and trap him, and he slices right through 'em. We walk into opposing gyms, and the people jeer at both of us.

Our team is super fun to watch. Greg is the speed dribbler, and I am the high-flying finisher. We get a couple of alley-oops every game, and the place goes bananas. No other team does that. All I have to do is give Greg a look, and he throws it exactly where I can get it. I won't have one lob dunk during my two seasons in college, but I have two or three every game in high school because of Greg.

My running and jumping ability is the most natural part of my game. It's not something I work at specifically, but it separates me even further from other players. I am pretty tall for a guard, but I can also *elevate*. That means I can get my shot off anytime I want. The only question is whether the ball is going in. Throw in the thousands of hours I have watched basketball on TV with my dad and absorbed the nuances of the game without even knowing it, and you have a very effective combination.

People don't expect a guy who looks like me to be able to jump so high. One time I am at a party with some buddies on a nearby farm. I don't smoke or drink, but everyone else there is pretty shit-faced. One reason I don't party like that is because Greg doesn't drink at all. Not even a drop. He gives me confidence that people can still have fun without it. Somehow it comes up that I can dunk a basketball, and a bunch of the kids there don't believe it. I laugh at them and say, "I could jump over that car right now, no problem." They insist I am full of shit, so we make a bet. I go outside, jump over the car like it is a box of matches, and collect the cash. That becomes one of our favorite party tricks with me and my buddies.

A lot of the parties we go to are out in rural areas. I even see a couple of cockfights. You go out to this big bonfire, and there are a couple of good ole boys who raised birds to fight one another. Everyone gathers in the barn and bets on the outcome. I don't like those fights, but that is just part of the culture. It's been going on for generations. There isn't much else to do out in the sticks.

I don't quite realize it, but the reactions to my style—and skin color—are starting to become a thing. Most of the time the comments are good-natured, but there are some bad exceptions. After we win a game at McLean County High School, we are coming out of the locker room when this man comes out of the stands to speak with me. He is big and gruff-looking, and he has a long ZZ Top–style beard. He puts his arm on my back like he has known me all his life.

"I love watching you play," he says. "You play just like a nigger, but you get to be white."

It is the worst thing I have ever heard. I look at the man, shocked, but he keeps right on smiling. There are a dozen or so adults standing around, and I know they heard what he said. I wait for one of them to object, but they are silent. A few of them think it is funny. I don't say anything in return. Just walk out and get on the bus.

I am confused and taken aback at first, but when I think about it later, I start to get really angry. He didn't say, "You're white." He said, "You *get* to be white." And he said it with such ease and comfort to someone he had never met before, with no effort to say it quietly.

In that moment, it dawns on me that for some people, maybe for a lot of people, the fact that I am a white guy who plays like a Black guy—and is beating the Black guys—is a big reason they cheer so hard for me. I try not to dwell on it, but that revelation messes with my mind, big-time. It makes me hate them almost as much as I love playing.

● ○ ●

My dad doesn't get to see me play a lot in high school because he is busy with his teams at Kentucky Wesleyan. That is a blessing in many ways. On the few occasions when he does come to a game, he chews me out afterward. He does not believe in giving compliments—at all.

One of the few times he sees me play is on the road against Butler County. We are supposed to beat 'em by 50, but only win by 15 or so. Still, I probably have 45 points, 18 rebounds, and 8 blocks. Riding home on the bus, I think, *He's gonna have to say something good about this one.*

I walk into our house, and Dad is sitting in the living room, smoking a cigarette, eating a sandwich that my mom made for him, drinking a Coke, looking at the TV. I come in and he says nothing. I shut the front door hard to make sure he knows I am there. Not a word. I walk over to my mom and ask, "Is something wrong with him?" She says she doesn't know.

I go into the living room and sit in his line of sight so he has to see me. Still, nothing. I finally speak up. "So what did you think?"

"Oh, you want to know what I think?" he asks. "I want to know when you're gonna take a fucking charge."

He gets out of his chair and says, "Get up." He is ready to run me right over. My mom dashes into the living room and puts an end to our conversation. A little while later she comes into my room to console me, but I don't want to hear it. "If he doesn't tell me what he thinks, how am I ever gonna know?" I say.

Finally, I tell him, "You know what? Don't come to my games anymore." I am a lot more relaxed when he isn't there, but I play harder when he is. I have games where I score 25 easy, but I should have gotten 50. The difference is, he isn't judging me based on what he sees in that moment. He is trying to prepare me for what is coming.

My mom might play peacemaker at home, but when she is at my games, she is for sure the craziest person in the gym. She sits in the bleachers with her girlfriends, smoking cigarettes and giving the refs all kinds of hell. One time I am jogging off the court at halftime, and I look up to see her leaning over a railing to get as close to the ref as possible. "Put on your fucking glasses, you bald-headed son of a bitch!" she shouts.

The ref shakes his head at me and says, "Your mom . . ."

● ○ ●

I try to ignore my dad when he gets on me, but I almost always listen to his advice, especially when it comes to basketball. One thing he always says is that girls are a distraction. I believe him—to a point.

Early in my sophomore year, we play a game against a team from Miami. One of the players has a dad who is loaded, so he paid to fly the whole team and their cheerleaders to Kentucky. We beat 'em pretty bad, but they still come back the next year. I am playing my usual game and having fun, but I also make a point to flirt with one of their cheerleaders during dead balls and time-outs. She is a supercute Black girl, and she flirts right back. By the end of the game, I know what room she is staying in at the Executive Inn. After the game, a few of us go over there to hang out with their team, and she and I hook up.

We exchange phone numbers and stay in touch all through the winter. The girl gives me numbers to use for a calling card so the calls won't show up on my parents' phone bills. I figure it is foolproof . . . until one day my folks get a bill for about two thousand bucks.

They are *pissed*. My dad has that look of disappointment you hate to see. He tells me I will have to work to pay him back, which seems impossible. The worst part is when he says to me, "Maybe you should just go down there and play for Miami." That hurts.

I show my mom a picture of the girl. I think Mom will be impressed, but instead she says, "Well, you know a lot of people around here would have a problem with that."

I am floored. I didn't think there was anyone who was better when it came to race than my parents. My mom tells stories about her father, who was a lawyer and represented Black families in Kentucky back in the 1960s. They had a few incidents where people burned crosses in their yard or planted Confederate memorabilia. My parents tell me and my sister over and over again, "We don't see color."

I know my mom has no problem with me dating a Black girl. But she knows that *other* people won't like it, so, well, maybe it isn't a good idea.

My life is about to get a lot more complicated because, for the first time, I really like a girl. And she is Black.

Her name is Shawn Higgs. Her older brother, Mark, is a great athlete who will go on to play in the NFL. Shawn lives near that Fifth Street neighborhood where I used to play all the time. She is funny, she is beautiful, and she is a great athlete. She wins the state high school championship in the 100 meters.

I've always thought Shawn was smoking hot, but she seems untouchable. She usually dates older guys. For a while she was with my buddy Chucky Taylor, but when he goes off to college, I decide it is time to make my move. I am shaking when I dial her up. When Shawn answers, I nervously ask if she will go out with me. She says no. I am crushed.

I find out later that she thought I was playing a trick on her. We have a friend who pranks people on three-way calls. Once she figures out I am serious, she agrees to a date. Within a few weeks we are fully together. Whether we are messing around or sitting on a couch quietly watching TV, Shawn and I are connected.

When it comes to spending time together, we don't have a whole lot of options. We certainly can't go out to dinner together or hold hands where a lot of other people are around. We never talk about why. So we hang out at her parents' house or an apartment where her older sister stays.

Shawn is a cheerleader at Owensboro High. Whenever we play them, she is right there cheering for the other team. That makes the games even more fun for me.

It isn't just white folks who have a problem with us dating. A lot of Black people aren't crazy about it, either. I am angry and confused. Why is it okay to like one kind of people but not another?

One morning the phone rings real early at the house. I go back to sleep, and when I wake up I hear my parents talking in the kitchen. My mom is real upset, and my dad is trying to calm her down. Turns out some stranger had called, and when she picked up the phone he asked, "What's white and comes in a black box?"

"I don't know," my mom answered.

"Your son," the man said. He hung up.

When she tells me what happened, I snicker. I think it is hilarious. My parents sure don't, though. My dad tries to brush it off, but my mom is rattled.

The idea that there is racism in our community is not exactly a revelation. One day our new US senator, Mitch McConnell, visits the high school. We walk onto the football field to meet the helicopter that will bring him in. The chopper arrives, Mitch gets out, and an aide steps off right behind him carrying a briefcase with a sticker of a Confederate flag. I know exactly what that flag stands for. Every time I pass one with my parents, they make a comment about how dumb it is. It's one thing for one of our neighbors to be flying that flag or putting a bumper sticker on their truck. But a guy working so closely with a US senator? And to have him put it in a place where everyone could see it like it was totally normal?

I walk right off that football field and head back toward the school. A bunch of teachers are lingering toward the back of the crowd smoking cigarettes. As I walk by, I look at them and say, "Fuck this guy." I have to serve three days of detention for cursing, but it's worth it.

Interracial couples are not unheard of where I am from, but they are definitely unusual. There are all sorts of double standards about it, too. It is always a Black man and a white woman, as far as I can tell. If there are instances of the opposite, I never see it. When I was living in Hawesville, there was a white teacher at my school who was married to a Black guy. She was treated so poorly by everyone, it was fucking gross. So I know the deal.

Shawn and I do our best to ignore the chatter, but it gets to us. We break up for a little while, but I think that is stupid, so we get back together. We do the only thing that seems to make sense, which is to hang out as much as we can and be seen by as few people as possible. The whole thing makes me angry and sad because we both understand the dynamic at play. The reason people think our relationship is a problem is because I am "lowering" myself by dating a Black girl. I can't imagine how much that hurts Shawn. This is what it means to be a Black person in Kentucky in the mid-1980s. Yeah, the situation is hard for me, too, but at least I get to be white.

● ○ ●

My college recruitment escalates during my junior year. I am not allowed to take official college visits or host coaches in my home; coaches are not allowed to contact me yet. But during my junior season, they are allowed to come watch me play. It is exciting, but I put a lot of pressure on myself. When I was growing up, I knew of a lot of guys who were highly thought of at some point, only to flame out for a variety of reasons. I don't want that to happen to me.

Most of the time I am not sure who is showing up or when. Sometimes they come to a game, or sometimes they watch me play pickup. North Carolina coach Dean Smith is one of the coaches who comes to watch me, in an open gym workout on Halloween. I always dress up as a woman for Halloween, and for some stupid reason I wear a long-haired wig and headband during that whole workout. Play my ass off, too. Some of my buddies suggest maybe that isn't the best idea considering there are college coaches in the gym, but I don't know enough to care.

Obviously, nearly everyone I know is a big Kentucky fan, but I know for certain that there is no way I am going to go there. They play this boring, slow, walk-it-up style of basketball, and I want absolutely no part of it. My grandmother, Mayme Hamby, lives in Lexington and she is good friends with Joe B. Hall, the Kentucky coach. I assume he knows there is no way I am going to play for him, so he doesn't come around much.

The University of Louisville, on the other hand, really appeals to me. I idolize Darrell Griffith, and I love the run-and-gun style that their coach, Denny Crum, plays. It looks like a perfect fit for me. Denny and his assistants, Wade Houston and Jerry Jones, are at almost every high school game of mine. Coaches from other schools show up, too, but most of the time I don't know who they are or where they are from. Crum has a great way of communicating, and I tell him I can't wait to play for him. I am all but committed.

I finish out my junior season. We end up being one of the top teams in the state again. I am really looking forward to the state tournament, which is played in Rupp Arena. It's the first time I have ever played a game there. We win our first game easily, but in the next round I deflect a pass on defense in the second half and break my right index finger. I try to play through the pain, but I can't do anything with the ball, and we end up losing. I am really pissed because we had a great chance to win a state championship.

A few weeks later, Kentucky's season ends with a loss to St. John's in the Sweet 16 of the NCAA tournament. I watch the game at home. Immediately after it is over, my phone rings. "Hey, Rex, this is Mr. Hagan," the voice says. It is Cliff Hagan, UK's athletic director. "I'm calling because I wanted you to know that Joe B. is going to announce his retirement in the next few minutes. We're going to hire Lute Olson or Eddie

Sutton. After we make our choice, I'm hoping you'll come down here for an official visit in the fall. What do you say?"

My first instinct is to let him know that I already told Denny that I am going to Louisville. Mr. Hagan is from my hometown, so I've known him a while. But I respect him too much to do that. "Yes, sir," I say.

"Okay, then, we'll be in touch tomorrow," he replies.

I hang up the phone and feel really upset. My dad's team has a game that night, so he doesn't get home until late. I tell him what happened. He tells me to call Coach Crum first thing in the morning and let him know what's going on.

I am terrified, but I make the call. "Hey, Coach, I just wanted you to know that Mr. Hagan called me last night, and I told him I would take an official visit to Kentucky," I say. "But don't worry, I'm still coming to Louisville."

Denny doesn't object in the least. "You need to do that for yourself, Rex," he says. That only makes me like him more.

chapter

4

I n the spring of 1985, my dad gets promoted to head coach at Kentucky Wesleyan. That summer, he takes his team to Europe for ten days. My mom and sister go with him. They make the brilliant decision to leave me in Owensboro. I am supposed to stay at a friend's house, but, as usual, I have my own ideas.

It's no coincidence that I start getting real rebellious at the same time I am coming into my own as a basketball player. I know deep down that the only thing I really care about is playing, and nobody is going to take that away. I have just gotten my driver's license, and when my family leaves for Europe, my cousin loans me her dad's brand-new, cherry-red Corvette Stingray.

I climb into the car, pick up Greg and the Vanderpool twins, and they squeeze into the tiny excuse for a backseat. I have been inseparable from those guys ever since we played peewee football together. A few other guys—Jeff Sanford, Danny Smith, David Helmers, and Barry Bartlett—hang out with us all the time, too. Everyone calls us the Fellas.

So here I am, cruising around Owensboro, when a buddy of mine pulls up in his Trans Am next to us at a stoplight. He revs his engine and says, "Run 'em?"

Fuck yeah.

The light turns green and this dude peels out. I race after him. I am a new driver, so I have no idea what I am doing. I don't go but a few hundred feet when I see police lights in my rearview mirror. *Ohhhh shit.* My parents are in Europe, my uncle has no idea I'm driving his car, and as this cop comes up to my window, my friends are hysterically laughing.

She taps on the window. I roll it down, scared shitless. The cop later writes on her report that I was speeding, driving recklessly, and eluding an officer. That last part isn't true. She adds in the report, "The occupants in the car thought the situation was quite comical." That is *definitely* true. I end up having to go to court and get sentenced to fifty hours of community service.

I know I will be in a shit ton of trouble when my parents get home. That is a scary thought. I am *so* scared that I wait all of two days before secretly flying off to Miami to see my cheerleader pal. Only a few of my closest friends know what I am doing. I have mowed enough yards to save a few hundred bucks for the plane ticket.

I fly out of Evansville. When I get to Miami, I stay at the

girl's house and even sleep in her room. Her parents seem okay with it. They know I am a big-time basketball player, all swagger and rocking a gold chain. I stay a couple of days and fly home. Somehow, my parents never find out about any of it.

Later that summer, I go to Europe myself with a team called the Kentucky All-Stars, which includes the best rising seniors in the state. We have a really good squad. There are ten of us on there who end up playing Division I. We go on a two-week trip to Iceland, England, France, and Germany.

I don't have much time at home before I head back out to attend Five-Star Basketball Camp near Pittsburgh. I really don't feel like going, but the camp's legendary founder, Howard Garfinkel, convinces me. I have studied all the recruiting rankings, so I am familiar with the top players in my class. This is my chance to see them in person.

Rumeal Robinson, who will later win a national championship at Michigan, is the biggest name coming into the camp. He is strong as shit and really quick, but I am full of confidence. All those little things my dad taught me from when I was young really stand out in a setting like this. Everyone at the camp has talent, but my knowledge and feel for the game separate me. I get pissed off when Rumeal gets named camp MVP, so I play as hard as I can in the all-star game and get named MVP of that. By the time I get home, every recruiting expert has me ranked in the top five of the senior class.

The last thing I do that summer is go with my grassroots

team to a tournament in Las Vegas. That is the first time a lot of folks out west see me play. Our team kills it, and I win the dunk contest.

Starting on July 1, college coaches are finally allowed to call me directly. The night before, I walk out of my house and see Jim Valvano, who is the coach at NC State, sitting in a car. I go up to say hello, but he motions at his watch. "It's not midnight yet," he says.

Sure enough, at the stroke of midnight, there is a knock at the door. It is Jimmy V, determined to be my first home visit. We invite him in and, true to his reputation, he is quite the charmer. "Everybody's gonna tell you the same thing, Rex," he says. "Let me ask you. What do you want to study?"

I shrug. "I dunno. Probably business."

He slaps me lightly in the face. "Great! We got the best business school in the world at North Carolina State! You're gonna love our business school!" He laughs and says, "Everybody's gonna say that. You watch."

I narrow my list to five schools—Louisville, Kentucky, North Carolina, Georgia Tech, and Western Kentucky. Indiana has been recruiting me, too. The night before I go public with my final five, Bob Knight calls to ask me when I am coming to visit. I start to explain to him that I have cut my choices to five and Indiana isn't on it, but after I get the first few words out, he hangs up on me.

My mom and dad sit in on all the home visits. There isn't much to talk about, since in my mind it is a foregone conclusion I am going to Louisville. Dean Smith comes with two of his assistants at North Carolina, Bill Guthridge and Roy Williams. My dad likes Dean a lot. He also knows Dean is a big smoker, so about a half hour into the visit, he says, "Dean, you wanna go have a cigarette?"

"Do I," Dean says. The two of them go on the porch, smoke, and talk for about forty-five minutes.

I mention during that visit that I am a big fan of Michael Jordan. He has been in the league for two years, and he is clearly a future star. A few days later, the phone rings. Jenny picks it up. "Can I talk to Rex?" the voice says.

"Who's calling?" she asks.

"Michael Jordan."

She figures it is a prank and hangs up.

Michael calls back and convinces her it is really him. She hands me the phone, and we speak for about ten minutes. It is cool to talk to him, but I know I'm not going to North Carolina.

It doesn't take long for Jenny to start resenting all of this. I can't say I blame her. Jenny is beautiful and athletic in her own right—our whole childhood, she could run faster than me—but I am treated like the golden child. The phone calls are the worst for her. There is only one phone line for the entire house. Call-waiting has just become a thing, so if Jenny is on a call with a friend and a coach clicks in, she has to end her conversation. That's about the worst thing you can do to a teenage girl. It becomes a running joke—*Jenny can't use the phone!*—but she doesn't think it is funny.

When we were real young, I thought Jenny was the prettiest, funniest little thing I'd ever seen. There's nothing I loved more than making her laugh. She was always more of a rebel than I was. I didn't like arguing with my dad because I was afraid of him, but Jenny always spoke her mind whether he liked it or not.

One day I am sitting in the cafeteria at our high school, and I hear people yelling, "Fight! Fight!" A scuffle has broken out, and just like everyone else, I run over to get a good look. I find Jenny putting a headlock on another girl, and she is just pummeling her. At this point, Jenny and I are barely speaking. We pass each other in the hallway at home and don't say a word. But she is still my kid sister, so I jump in and pull her off. Jenny shoves me hard, scratching my face pretty bad.

"Get off me, you fucking dick!" she shouts.

She goes back to fighting, but the teachers break it up. I find out later the reason the fight started was because this other girl called me a dick. That's Jenny for you. She can call me a dick all she wants, but if someone else does it, there is gonna be trouble.

● ○ ●

I want to take all my campus visits early in the fall and get my decision over with so I can enjoy my senior season. Those trips open my eyes to what it really means to be a big-time basketball recruit. I have some basic understanding that there is cheating going on with respect to NCAA rules, but I am so young and naïve I don't really think about it. I am just excited to be able to go to college and play ball. I don't need anything else.

A school tells my dad that it will put $500,000 in an escrow account for every year I play there. My dad tells me, but I don't want to go there, and besides, I have no idea what an escrow account is. While I don't have people outright saying they can give me cash or a car or a stereo or whatever, I definitely get the sense that I can have that conversation if I want to. During my visits, the players say vague things like "They take care of us here." I see guys who are driving cars and using stereos in their rooms I doubt they can afford.

When I tell my dad about what is going on, I expect him to tell me not to go to those places. But he doesn't. That is a surprise because he has always told me that cheaters are bad. I am puzzled he's not more pissed off. I probably should be more disappointed in him, but the truth is I am driving a shitty 1966 Volkswagen, and I like the idea of upgrading my ride. Whatever other stuff comes along with that, that is fine by me.

The only reason I have Georgia Tech on my list is because one of their players, Craig Neal, is a real good friend and asks me to visit. It ends up being my best college visit. Bobby Cremins, the Georgia Tech coach, takes me to the Martin Luther King Center along with Craig, John Salley, and Bruce Dalrymple. We spend a couple hours walking around and reading everything. It is so interesting.

If I hadn't made that promise to Mr. Hagan, I would never have visited Kentucky. I am a Louisville Cardinal all the way. My mindset starts to change when Eddie Sutton, who got the nod as Joe B. Hall's successor, taps Dwane Casey to be his assistant. Dwane was a childhood hero of mine. I grew up watching him play for Union County High School and then at UK. When he was through playing, Case coached at Western Kentucky under Clem Haskins. My dad and Clem are real tight, so when I was in middle school, I would go to basketball camps at Western Kentucky, where Case coached me a bunch. I hung out at Clem's house a bunch with my parents and got to be buddies with his daughter Clemette. She was two years older than me and we kissed a few times, but she also beat my ass in basketball, which drove me crazy. She went on to play at WKU and was a three-time all-American. When I started getting recruited in high school, I told everyone that Western Kentucky was one of my finalists as a favor to my dad. I knew I wasn't gonna go there, but now that Case has been hired at Kentucky, it gets my attention. I'm not saying that's the reason Eddie hired Dwane—but I'm not saying it's *not* the reason. I am a very high-profile in-state player, and it would be pretty bad for Kentucky to let me go to another school, especially if that school is Louisville.

Eddie had never really seen me play before he got the Kentucky job, so he has a lot of catching up to do. Soon after getting hired, Eddie wants to come see me play in an open gym, but I don't have any gyms to play in. Case finds out that I play at Legion Park almost every day. One night, we are about to play under the lights, and I look over and see him and Eddie standing on the side along with the other assistant, James Dickey. I put on a show that night as I always do. After that, Eddie has no doubt that he wants to recruit me.

Before my visit, Dwane does something smart. He asks

if I want Reggie Hanson to come with me. Reggie is a really good player at Pulaski County High School in Somerset, Kentucky. We have played together at a bunch of camps and all-star games, and he was on my team that went to Europe over the summer. Reggie is my buddy, and he is considered the second-best player in the state. As far as I know, Kentucky isn't even recruiting him, but I think he is good enough to play there.

The visit takes place on a football weekend in the fall. Dwane picks me and Reggie up from the airport and takes us straight to Wildcat Lodge, where the basketball players live. I had been told it's a men's-only dorm, and that women are absolutely not allowed. Then I get inside, and girls are everywhere. That gets my interest.

They call it a lodge for a reason. It looks like a fancy hotel you'd see in Aspen. The players have eight-foot beds, big-screen TVs, and a full-time cook. *Shit*, I think, *I could get used to this*. Then the coaches take me on a tour of Rupp Arena, which I had seen before and actually played in once during the state tournament. But to visit under these circumstances has a whole new impact. For the first time, I envision what it would be like to play at Kentucky.

Three players, Kenny Walker, Winston Bennett, and Ed Davender, take us to the football game. The team is bad, but there are still forty thousand people there. It seems like everyone in the stadium knows who I am. People are calling out to me left and right, saying how much they want me to be a Wildcat.

I finally get it: *If I come here, I'll be a rock star.*

All the things that shouldn't matter, matter. Louisville can't compete with that. No school can. I also realize that if you play for the University of Kentucky, you're loved in that state for the rest of your life. A lot of former UK players still live there and benefit from all that goodwill when it comes to looking for jobs and other things. I feel like I can always count on that safety net.

Dwane rides with me on the flight back to Owensboro. He keeps asking me, "What can we do?" I mention again how much I like Reggie and how good I think he is. "You want Reggie to come?" Dwane asks. "You guys can room together."

I tell him that sounds great. "Done," he says. The next day, Kentucky offers Reggie a scholarship. I never promised I would come if they did that, but it definitely makes UK more appealing.

A couple of weeks later, I take my official visit to Louisville. Three of their players, Kenny Payne, Robbie Valentine, and Pervis Ellison, are my hosts. I stay at a local hotel. It is a nice place, but it isn't Wildcat Lodge. I had a blast on that visit, but in the end, I choose Kentucky. It is all pretty surprising considering I grew up hating their teams, but I fall for the whole seduction of the place. I call Denny the night before my official announcement to let him know my decision. He accepts the news with grace and class. I am so thankful for that.

The next day, I stand before a crowded classroom with a low ceiling and a row of microphones. I am wearing a gold chain on top of my gray sweater and big glasses that are 100 percent fake. I guess I think if I am wearing glasses, people will assume I am smart. All they really care about is whether I am going to Kentucky. When I break the news, the room erupts in applause. The intensity of the reaction takes me by surprise. Until that point, I hadn't quite realized just how badly all those people wanted me to play for UK. I have to eat shit from a lot of my buddies 'cause I had trashed the Cats for so long. But they're all Kentucky fans, so they're happy.

● ○ ●

The spotlight gets brighter than ever. People camp out the night before our games so they can get tickets. The stands are packed so tight that the fire marshals have to clear people out. The gyms are thick with cigarette smoke.

I hear myself being compared often to former Wildcats. Kyle Macy is the one I hear the most. I also hear a lot of comparisons to non-Kentucky players like Pete Maravich and Jerry West. No doubt those guys were great players, but I don't know anything about them except that they are white. That bugs me because I think of myself more like Darrell Griffith and NC State's David Thompson, the two guys I idolize the most. Both of them are killer athletes who attack the rim with abandon. I try to imitate them every time out.

But that's how it is in sports. White guys are compared to white guys, and Black guys are compared to Black guys. It is a pattern that will recur throughout my career and bother me to no end.

The highlights of my senior season are the games against Owensboro High. These games are wars, man. Owensboro's arena seats about fifty-five hundred, but for these games they squeeze in more than six thousand. All the Owensboro guys were my teammates during summer ball. Greg and I get great satisfaction out of going up against them and showing our Apollo teammates how to compete at that level. I tell them, "If you think you're beat, you're beat." It occurs to me numerous times that season that Greg is good enough to play for Kentucky, too. He should be coming with me to Lexington.

I get double- and triple-teamed, but it doesn't matter. Like George Gervin used to say, I am gonna get my 35 no matter what they do. The only question is whether it is gonna be a hard 35 or an easy 35. It depends on how hard the other team is gonna fight me. Well, no one fights me harder than Owensboro, and they have the talent to do it. They're not scared of me, either. I played Owensboro ten times during my last two years of high school, and we went 5-5. Those games prepare me for the rigors of college ball as well as anything can. I score a ton of points and smile at Shawn, who stands on the baseline in her cheerleading outfit looking cute as can be.

Owensboro brings out the best in me, and sometimes the worst. We play them in a Christmas tournament and are down by 4 points in the fourth quarter. We are fighting like hell to come back, but then the coach takes me out to tell me something. In the brief time I sit out, Owensboro scores again. The coach, John Whitmer, hurries me back to the scorer's table, but it takes another minute and a half for play to stop. By the time I get back in, we are down 12. This is before the three-point line, too. It feels like we're down 30.

I am so pissed, I go on strike. If someone throws me the ball, I throw it back. The coach calls time-out, and I say to him, "I wouldn't put me back in if I were you." He doesn't. We lose.

As soon as I get in the locker room, I cut off my tape, throw my clothes in my bag, and walk out. The coach asks me where I am going.

"I quit," I say.

"You quit?" he replies. "You're quitting on these guys?"

"No, I love these guys. I'm quitting on you."

When my dad comes home, I tell him what I've decided. He about laughs me out of the house. "You didn't quit," he says. "You're going to Kentucky, and you just quit your high school team. You think that's going to be all right?"

"I don't care what anyone thinks," I say. "This is not my fault. I'm done."

The next morning before school, we have a meeting at the coach's house with him and his assistant. It's awkward because he used to be my dad's assistant coach, and he lives right next door to us. "I want to come back to the team," I say.

"Fine," the coach says. "But we're gonna suspend you for a game."

I agree. We tell everyone I sat out because I have the flu.

● ○ ●

For Christmas that year I get a brand-new car, a sweet, black Camero IROC-Z28 with T tops and a custom stereo. My dad goes down to the dealer and picks it out for me. My sister gets a nice little new black car as well. You'd think me going from driving a beat-up old Volkswagen Beetle to that slick machine would raise suspicions, but nobody gives a shit. They call it the IRex.

The scariest moment for me that season happens after a game at Breckinridge County High School. That's the school we were playing the year before when I broke that kid's nose. As I head out toward the bus after the game, there is a crowd of people, and I notice a man moving toward me in an aggressive fashion. He is a big, scraggly guy. I look down at his hand and see that he has a knife. Fortunately, some people who are standing there wrestle him to the ground and shove me onto the bus.

As luck would have it, we draw Owensboro in our first game of the district tournament. We are two of the best teams in the state, but the tournament is bracketed not based on seeding, but on a random draw, which is a shitty way of doing things. The Owensboro Sportscenter is jam-packed as always, and we take an 8-point lead into the final three minutes. We have the momentum until the clock malfunctions and runs off time it shouldn't have. The scoreboard operator has to start from the beginning and run the time down. And then he messes it up and has to do it again.

The long delay takes away our momentum. When play resumes, we are tight and they are aggressive. They are fouling to try to come back, and my teammates miss two front ends of one-and-ones. They miss a shot, and I am fouled on the rebound. I go to the foul line 100 percent confident I'll make two shots and ice the game.

I miss.

We are up one with ten seconds to go. A guy on their team named Orlando Stewart, who is one of my AAU teammates, sinks a seventeen-foot shot to give them the lead with four seconds left. We call time-out. Then I get the ball, dribble upcourt, and let fly a half-court shot.

Clank. Game over. High school career over. Total devastation.

I don't have time to wallow in my sorrow. The basketball whirlwind continues through the spring when I play in the McDonald's All American Game, by far the most prestigious national showcase, as well as the Derby Festival Classic. That game is a big deal in Kentucky. Reggie Hanson plays in it, too, and he and I are roommates at the hotel. We like to do really smart things together like play with fire. We light matches and flick them at each other. One of the matches lands on a lampshade, and before we can put out the fire, it spreads to the curtains and up the ceiling. The sprinklers come on across the entire floor and we run out into the hallway screaming, "Fire! Fire!" The fire department comes and puts it out.

I think for sure they are gonna send us home, but that doesn't happen. Apparently, they need me to play more than they need me not to burn down the hotel.

A few days later, Reggie and I are roommates again, this

time for the Kentucky-Indiana All-Stars games. This is a two-week event with two games in Kentucky and one in Indiana. It includes boys' and girls' teams. These games are the first time I ever play with a three-point line, which had been used in college for the first time that season. Not only does it give me an extra point for shots I was already making, but it forces the defenses to guard me really close out there, which makes it that much easier to drive. We smoke Indiana in the first game, and when it is over, someone hands me a stat sheet. I thought I had maybe 30 points, but I actually had closer to 37 because of that line.

Most of the other players go home between games, but Reggie and I want to stay at the hotel. There are a couple of girl players who are also staying there, and we are quite interested in getting to know them better.

The problem is that we are all on a curfew, and there are security people keeping an eye on us. No problem! Reggie and I figure we will just climb out our window, shimmy down the ledge, and sneak into the girls' room. This ledge is maybe eight inches wide and we are on the fourth floor. We climb onto the ledge and slide inside the girls' room.

At that very moment, their coach walks in. We panic and scurry back out the window and climb to the roof, but it is too late. The coach sticks his head out the window and cusses us out. Once again, nobody says a word.

● ○ ●

The school year ends with my senior prom. It would be nice if I could take Shawn as my date, but that isn't an option. For that whole school year, she and I snuck around. Her parents converted their garage into a living space, so we spent a lot of time in there. Or we would go to her sister's place across town.

My parents know full well that she is my girlfriend, but we don't talk about her much. If one of our schools has a dance, we go with a friend and then meet up somewhere later that night. Going to a public event like a prom is absolutely out of the question. The whole thing fucking sucks.

Graduation day comes, and I am finally done with high school. Between the tension at home, the pressure of being a local celebrity, and the blowback I am getting from dating Shawn, I can't wait to get out of there. I pack up my stuff, say my goodbyes, and head for Lexington.

chapter

5

Freshmen aren't allowed to live on campus until school starts, so Reggie and I spend part of the summer of 1986 working on thoroughbred farms outside Lexington. I think it will be easy, but I am very wrong. We have to wake up early and then go dig postholes, hot walk horses, muck stalls, paint fences, or do whatever work they have for us that day.

Our apartment in Lexington is a one-room efficiency, but it feels like the Ritz-Carlton to us. We are the classic odd couple. He's a neat freak who irons his jeans. I never once make my bed. The basketball team is on an overseas trip that summer, so it is just the two of us those first few weeks. Once the rest of the guys get back, we add weight lifting and playing ball to our daily schedules. If I ever had any doubt that I wasn't in high school anymore, it is erased when those guys come back. In my mind, I have a long way to go before I am ready to be an effective college player.

When the summer ends, Reggie and I move into our room in Wildcat Lodge. We are the classic odd couple. He's a neat freak who irons his jeans. I never once make my bed. We are also pure trouble. If we aren't making it, we are finding it—and it is finding us. It doesn't take long, either. Right before our freshman year starts, I take Reggie to visit my grandmother in Lexington. We are driving back to the Lodge through a rough section of town, and I pull up to a stop sign. Right when we stop, a prostitute walks up to the car and asks Reggie to roll down his window. "Hey, fellas," she says. "Twenty dollars for a suck and fuck."

We think it is hilarious. I can't believe someone could be so bold. We are joking around with her when suddenly I hear a *whoop whoop* sound. I look in my rearview mirror and there is a police car with its hood lights twirling.

Ohhhh shit.

The girl opens the door and tries to jump in the car, but Reggie pushes her away. I turn the corner, as if getting out of the cops' way, hoping they aren't coming for us. But they are. They approach the car, and one of them asks for my license. I hand it over and can tell he knows who I am.

They put the prostitute in the police car, and a few minutes later the cop comes back. "What were y'all doing with that girl?" he asks.

"Officer," I say, "we weren't doing anything."

"She says she knows you."

"No, sir, we don't know her at all. We stopped at the stop sign and she came up to our car and started talking to us."

I just about shit myself, but he eventually believes us. The cop hands me back my license and says we can go home. It doesn't take but four minutes to drive back to Wildcat Lodge. We are still shaking when we get out of the car.

Who should be standing right there but Dwane Casey and the other assistant coach, James Dickey. Somehow, before cell phones, before the internet, they have gotten wind of what happened. They are not happy, but they believe our story. And they should, because this time, at least, we are telling the truth.

●　○　●

When I left home, I weighed about 160 pounds, tops. My dad thought they might redshirt me. He was concerned whether I would be physically ready to level up. "There are gonna be days when you come home and you hate your coach and the last thing you want to do is touch a basketball," he warned. "But just hang in there, and eventually those days will be few and far between."

Playing against the Kentucky guys in pickup games is a real eye-opener, just as my dad predicted. Skills-wise I feel like their equal, but they can go longer and harder than I can. I'll be feeling good at the start of our pickup games, but then I'll become exhausted. The weight room workouts are especially humiliating. When we start off bench-pressing, I can only lift the bar. Literally, they can't put any plates on it. We share the weight room with the football team, which doesn't help my self-esteem.

Another part of preseason conditioning is the drug test. They want to know who is smoking weed. I don't smoke, but some of the other guys do, so someone comes up with the idea to use my urine. I pee into a couple of small bottles and give it to some teammates. Come the day of the test, I go into the bathroom and step into the stall to fill my sample. I hear a sound.

Clink.

I look down. The vial I had given my teammate has hit the floor and is rolling out of the stall. All my pee spills out. He drops his sample cup, too, while attempting the exchange. We are busted.

The coaches scare the shit out of us. They tell us we are gonna be in all this trouble with the school. That doesn't happen, but they make us do extra conditioning work for a few weeks.

When fall comes around, Reggie and I move into rooms across the hall from each other. The coaches want me to live with Winston Bennett, who's a senior and is supposed to give me some veteran guidance. The Vanderpool brothers live there, too. This is another power move pulled off by Dwane. He knows how close I am with those guys, so he arranges for them to stay at the Lodge even though they aren't basketball players. I feel like an alien walking on campus, with people looking at me all the time and watching my every move. Those guys are like my security blanket and a constant source of comedy. One night I come back to the Lodge and see a few of my teammates standing in the parking lot watching Kevin and Keith fighting each other in the bushes. They had ordered a pizza and got into a brawl over who was supposed to pay the five bucks.

Once classes start, I feel I can hold my own, but my desire to succeed academically has its limits. I take a class with one of the other players. Two weeks in, we have our first big test. We both know there is no chance we will pass it. Fortunately, there is this band guy who sits next to us, and we assume he's way smarter than we are. We ask if we can cheat off him, and he is happy to help.

Test day comes, and we figure we are set. My teammate and I try to copy off this guy's paper discreetly. It is all going fine until about ten minutes in, when this other student gets up and hands in his test. My buddy and I look at each other in panic. We finish up as best we can.

Two days later, we get the tests back. There is so much red ink on them, it looks like someone bled all over the pages. On top of the papers, the teacher has written, "Whose idea was this? See me after class."

We meet with the teacher, and he is shaking his head. "What are you guys doing?" he says. "Do you realize you could get kicked out of school if I report this?"

Holy shit, am I scared. I think about having to call my parents. I think about all the headlines reporting I have been kicked out of UK for cheating.

"The question is, how are we going to fix this?" the

professor says. "I'll give you the weekend to come up with an answer."

Monday comes, and we meet with him again. Somehow I have been elected to speak for us and propose our solution. "How about if we give you tickets to the games and some autographed shoes and basketballs?"

The teacher looks at us in disbelief. "That's your answer? You're bribing me?"

So I take that as a no?

He would be justified to report us, but he comes up with his own solution. "You are going to be at every class and you are going to work hard to pass," he says. "You are going to do the work I ask you to do, and if I call on you, you are going to have a reasonable answer. You're not going to crack jokes and disrupt the class. And I have the basketball schedule. If you're not at a road game, you better be here and ready to work."

We agree to his terms. I get a C in the class. Nobody ever finds out.

● ○ ●

As practice officially gets under way in mid-October, I am honestly wondering whether I can play college basketball, at least right away. Those doubts don't last long. I realize just how much of an advantage I have from watching my dad's practices while growing up. During the very first practice, we are running offense. I make a simple post pass where I fake like I'm throwing high and then feed the big man low. I've done it a million times without thinking about it, but Eddie stops practice and shouts, "That's why he's the best player in here!" It makes me want to run and hide. I am the new kid with the big rep, and I want the older guys to accept me.

Ideally, you come into college with a pretty good relationship with the head coach, but that isn't the case with me and Eddie. He didn't spend much time recruiting me before I committed. He has only been here for one season, but he is already the toast of the town, having led UK to a 32-4 record and a trip to the Elite Eight. There is no doubt as to who is running the show. If we want minutes, we will have to fall in line.

That appears to be the message Eddie tries to deliver at one of our first practices. As we sit in our chairs, Eddie pulls out a box of rings commemorating all the Southwest Conference titles he won at Arkansas. "This is what we play for, guys," he drawls. "Anything short of an SEC championship is unacceptable."

I look around, wondering if this is supposed to be a prank. Unlike most of the other players, I grew up in Kentucky. I know the deal. An SEC championship doesn't mean shit to our fans. They only want one thing—a national championship. Anything less than *that* is unacceptable. I understand that, but I'm not sure Eddie does.

We go on a mini-tour around the state to play blue-white scrimmages. The arenas are packed. I am the one they swarm the most. I'm sure I look confident, but on the inside I am really insecure. I have always been a pleaser, so I do my best to interact because I am afraid to let anyone down. But if someone comes up to me and asks for an autograph, I won't even be able to look them in the eye. I just don't know any better.

We also play an exhibition against the Yugoslavian national team. They have several future NBA players in Toni Kukoč, Dražen Petrović, and Vlade Divac. I come off the bench and score a bunch of points, but I have no chance guarding Dražen, who's older and stronger than I am. It dawns on me that I am going to be going up against a lot of guards this season who are a lot stronger than I am.

● ○ ●

The season gets under way in November. Our third game is a big matchup at Indiana. The Hoosiers are ranked third in the country and will go on to win the national championship. Their best player is Steve Alford, a senior guard who was a preseason All-American and is a favorite for national player of the year. He's from Indiana, so I've been hearing about him for years.

I am interested to see how I will do against Steve. He is much more experienced and knows how to get open and run off a bunch of screens. He starts off guarding me, but I notice after a few possessions he's switched to a different player. Steve scores 26 points, but I score 26, too, and though we lose in overtime, 71–66, that game gives me a ton of confidence. I pass by Bob Knight on the way to the press conference. "I'm sorry I hung up on you when you were in high school," he says. It is nice of him, but I doubt he would have said it if we had won.

I play well in our next three games, too, which are all wins. That sets the stage for the massive showdown at Louisville on December 27. The Kentucky-Louisville rivalry is as big as there is in college basketball, especially with the Cardinals coming off that national championship. It is going to be the biggest game of my life by far.

And I almost don't play.

The day before we leave, I am in my room in Wildcat Lodge when there is a knock on my door after curfew. It is Dwane and James Dickey. I try to be all innocent—"Hey guys, what's going on?"—but they walk right past me and into my bedroom. They see I have a girl in there, which is not allowed.

Oops.

When the guys tell Coach Sutton what I have done, he immediately says, "He's not playing."

I am crushed. I know this is going to be huge news. The next day, however, Dwane calls me and says Eddie is offering me a choice. "You can sit out the game," he says, "or you can play and ride the bike at five in the morning every day for a couple of weeks."

Shit, that is an easy one for me. I am playing.

So we go to Louisville, have the open practice, and check into a local hotel. I have a hard time sleeping that night because my roommate, Richard Madison, is a full-fledged insomniac. The dude never sleeps. I wake up at six in the morning because he is doing push-ups and watching *The*

Flintstones on TV. He has a thing for Betty Rubble. We have to get up soon anyway, and I am too wired to go back to sleep, so I figure I will put on my sweats and walk around the hotel.

I go to get on the elevator. When the doors open, I come face-to-face with Eddie. He is wearing a trench coat and has glass bottles of Absolut vodka sticking out of his pockets. He is hammered.

"Rex?" he says. "What are you doing up?"

"I couldn't sleep, Coach," I reply.

"Go on back to your room."

Later that day, with the arena packed and a national TV audience watching on CBS, I score 26 points in an 85–51 win. It is a great day, but it crushes me to see Denny Crum lose. He is all class afterward, just like always.

On my way back from the postgame press conference, someone comes into the locker room and says, "The champ wants to say hi." I have no idea what he is talking about until I walk out. There stands Muhammad Ali, waiting patiently for the chance to meet me.

From that point on, Lexington is *Rexington*, and I am King Rex. Oh, and those early-morning bike rides that were supposed to be my punishment? They never happen.

● ○ ●

I can go home for a few days over Christmas break. Before I leave, one of my favorite boosters approaches me and hands me an envelope full of cash. "Give this to your dad," he says. I don't ask what the money is for, but I assume it is reimbursement for the IRex, which I find out later was bought by my uncle E.L. My dad takes it without saying a word.

Apparently, we get a little too full of ourselves after thumping Louisville, because three days later, we lose to unranked Georgia. We win at fifth-ranked Auburn in our next game, but then lose the next two to Alabama and Tennessee. Eddie is not happy. He has already signed the best recruiting class in the country coming for next season. When he gets mad, Eddie will tell us, "Just wait til y'all see the troops we got coming in next year. You will *not* see the floor." I doubt he is directing that at me, but even if he is, it doesn't bother me. I know that no one is taking my spot.

Eddie hardly ever chews me out. It can get real awkward when he blasts the older guys and doesn't say but a couple words to me. There are plenty of times I deserve to get criticized, but for the most part, he lays off.

I am starting to be game-planned by opposing teams. They have their guys get physical with me and crowd my space. In the open floor I can play with anyone, but if I don't have room, I am a lot less effective. It works sometimes, but I almost never have two bad games in a row. Win or lose, I am back in the gym for hours getting ready for the next one.

By the middle of January, the King Rex story has gone national. Pete Maravich comes to interview me for a TV network. I even make the cover of *Sports Illustrated*. Well, not the *full* cover, just a little box on the top right corner. I was supposed to get the full cover, but then Brian Bosworth got busted for steroids and bumped me. That week we go to Starkville to play Mississippi State. It is a national TV game, so the network sends Cheryl Miller in a day early to do a story on me. She has recently finished up playing for USC and is working as a sideline reporter. We sit down for the interview and then spend some time talking. I am smitten.

Cheryl happens to mention she is staying at the same motel we are staying at. Later that night, I am in my room talking to my roommate about Cheryl, and we hatch a plan for me to try to go visit her. The problem is that we have to be in our rooms for bed checks. After someone comes by to make sure we are all tucked in, I wait about thirty minutes, climb onto the balcony, and slide down a pole. I knock on Cheryl's door and we hang out for a while. I climb back up the pole, go back to bed, and the next day we win the game.

Cheryl gives me her number back in LA, and I call her a bunch of times over the next few months. Her brother Reggie is playing for UCLA, and there are a couple of occasions when he picks up the phone. I definitely get the impression that Reggie is *not* feeling it. Many years later, when we face off in the NBA, it seems like Reggie goes at me extra hard. I always suspect it is because of all those calls to his sister.

● ○ ●

I take a psychology class my second semester. This is a bad idea. One day we get into a deep discussion about whether our psychological makeup is predetermined or whether we can change it through free will. Something about this class messes me up. I am not sure why, but it makes me feel really sad. The last thing I want to do is go deeper into my own head. Lotta dark shit going on in there. I ask the coaches to switch me out.

I have always been a bad sleeper, but as the season goes on, it seems things are getting worse. I mention this to one of our trainers, and he gives me a Valium. I sleep great that night and continue to use Valium.

The coaches keep a close eye on my studies, but I got a 3.2 grade point average that first semester, so they leave me alone. I wish I could say the same for my personal life. Shawn had enrolled at Kentucky the same time I did. My coaches are very interested in keeping tabs on that.

Everyone knows Shawn is my girlfriend. We make no effort to hide it. She lives in a dorm across the street, and we often walk to class together. Shawn and I don't talk about it, but I think we are both under the assumption that now that we have moved to a bigger city, people's attitudes about us hanging out together will be different. Dwane and the coaches who recruited me pretty much assured me of that.

I am working out at the Coliseum one day and get pulled into the head coach's office. Eddie is in there with Dwane and James. "You need to be careful about who you're spending time with," Eddie says. "We're not saying you can't, but you gotta be quiet about it. People are talking about it."

At first I think it is a joke. I am wrong. It is the same bullshit message I have heard before. *We don't have a problem with this, but other people will, so you better be careful.* I look over at Dwane, who is Black. He doesn't say anything, but he's nodding at me in a way that is trying to comfort me.

I walk out of there so disappointed and upset. I had thought Shawn and I were done dealing with this shit, but it is only starting up again. The worst part is now I have to go talk to Shawn about the conversation. I hope she will take it well, but she doesn't. I can see the tears welling in her eyes. It is crushing, for both of us. The issue isn't that we shouldn't be dating, it's that she's seen as not good enough to be dating me, which sucks, because as far as I'm concerned, I'm not good enough for anyone, much less Shawn. I can only imagine how she feels.

The meeting makes it even harder than usual to fall asleep that night. When I wake up the next morning, my body is overcome with sensations I have never felt before. My heart is racing. I can't catch my breath. Most frightening of all, I cannot lift my arms. I have them wrapped around my body.

I call out to Reggie, who is staying in Winston's room while Winston is back home in Louisville. "Reggie, wake up!" I say. "Something's wrong with me. Go get Dwane."

Reggie runs out of the room, and a short while later, he comes back in with Dwane. He can tell right away something is really wrong with me. I want to go to a hospital, but they are reluctant. What will people say? Dwane calls James and asks him to come pick me up. They get Shawn and take us to a nearby thoroughbred farm owned by Don and Linda Johnson, who are big supporters of the program. They are older and white, and they know all about me and Shawn. They absolutely do not give a shit, and I love them for that. For the next few days, Shawn and I stay with him and his wife until I feel better.

I miss two days of practice. Once I feel up to it, Dwane comes and gets me and takes me back to campus. He and James never say another word about what happened, and neither do I.

chapter

6

One of the most popular bars near campus is a place called Two Keys Tavern. A lot of the players like to go there, as does much of the student body. Technically, you need to be twenty-one to get in, but everyone has fake IDs, and the bouncers aren't strict.

One night after a workout, I go to Two Keys with the other players. I'm not a drinker, but I like to hang out. The other guys file inside one by one, but I get stopped at the door.

"Hey, Rex, I'm sorry, but I can't let you in," the bouncer says. "If people find out you were here, they'll call the cops and shut us down."

The next day, I ask Dwane for a key to the gym. If I'm not gonna be allowed to hang out in bars, I might as well be getting up shots. I spend a lot of nights in there by myself or with Reggie, or with someone else rebounding for me.

With little else to do during the day, I find myself sleeping—a lot. I'm done with class at 10:00 a.m. and don't have practice until 2:30. I sleep for a couple of hours, wake up, see it is only noon, and then go back to sleep.

I am living a surreal existence. I walk around campus and get swarmed by people who want autographs. The worst is having to deal with adults. On top of talking to the media, which I never enjoy, I have to wear a suit to all these official functions and schmooze with boosters. I am pretending to be a grown-up, but inside I feel like I am twelve.

Whatever problems I have, access to spending money isn't one of them. There are certain people who I see after a game, and I know to go over to them to say hi. By the time I walk out of the arena, my jacket pockets are stuffed with a few hundred bucks. Sometimes I get invited over to someone's house for dinner. I almost always walk out with money. If I need a few thousand bucks, I know who to ask. I can't exactly put all this cash in a bank. So I put it all in a shoebox and keep it under my bed. Reggie knows he can go in there any time and take whatever he needs. There is always more where that came from.

Since I am pretty much stuck in my dorm room by myself all the time, I figure I might as well invite in all the company I can. Chasing girls becomes my major. I have sex pretty much every day, often more than once. I'll go to class with swimmers and volleyball players, ask one of them if she wants to hang out, and pretty soon we are in her room, or my room, or maybe even a bathroom in an academic building.

I am scared shitless of getting someone pregnant, or worse, getting AIDS. The AIDS epidemic has just exploded, so it is drilled into everyone's head that you have to use protection. Sometimes I even wear two condoms, although I learn later on you're not supposed to do that. Much later in life, I get a couple calls from women who claim they had my child, but I know they are full of shit. I was too careful for that.

I am a terrible boyfriend. It is a challenge keeping all this from Shawn. She comes close to catching me a couple of times, but I somehow lie my way out of trouble. One night, she hears that I have a girl in my room at the Lodge, so she stands outside my room throwing rocks at my window, cussing up a storm. I get the girl out of there, go down to see Shawn, and claim innocence.

I am able to keep most of what I am doing from Shawn because the Black sororities and white sororities do not mingle with each other. I know that if I sleep with another Black girl on campus, Shawn will for sure find out about it, so I limit myself to white girls. I convince myself that if Shawn doesn't know what's going on, then it's no big deal.

Girls are a pleasant distraction. Chasing them also appeals to my competitive instincts. After I leave college, my buddies will tease me that they should retire my jersey in Wildcat Lodge. I take it as a compliment, but years later, especially when I have daughters of my own, I will understand it was nothing to be proud of.

● ○ ●

The shit I am actually doing with girls is bad enough, but on top of that there are tons of crazy rumors going around that are not true. People tell me they heard that I am sleeping with a teammate's girlfriend or sister, or that I have all these biracial kids living all over the state. It is out of control.

Soon after that conversation with Eddie and the coaches in his office, I find out people are keeping a real close eye on me. Managers follow me on campus and around town to see who I am hanging with. It feels like everyone is spying on me, including professors. I walk into practice and see Eddie say something to James. Then James walks over and asks, "Were you at the movies last night over at South Park?"

"Yeah."

"You better be careful."

One night I walk out of Rupp Arena with Reggie after a game. We make our way through the parking lot and come upon a group of fans who are milling around my car. When they see us, they take off running. I am confused until I walk to the car and see what they have done. The words "nigger lover" are keyed into the door.

I can't believe it. We just won a game. These are supposed to be our fans. I am hurt, angry, confused. My car is vandalized like that two more times while I'm at Kentucky.

I don't speak up about any of this, even though I have this huge platform, and my words would carry some weight. Every time I suggest to someone I might want to say something about what is going on, they reply, "But your image . . ." So I keep my mouth shut. I am only nineteen years old and not the most well-rounded kid. I get pretty good grades, but mostly because I am just smart enough to bullshit my way through my classes. The basketball part I can handle, but all the pressure and scrutiny that comes with it is too much. I am in a very fragile emotional state. The last thing I need is more controversy.

● ○ ●

Eddie Sutton is a brilliant coach and a decent man, but he is a serious alcoholic. I knew when I first got there that Coach wasn't in a great state of mind, but it takes me a while to realize just how bad things are.

One night I go into Memorial Coliseum real late with Reggie to get in a workout. We are walking down the hallway and spot two legs sticking out of one of the offices. We walk up to the legs and see it is Eddie, completely passed out on the floor. I am real scared. I think he must have had a heart attack or a stroke or something. I shout at Reggie to get Dwane, who lives at the Lodge.

Dwane comes running in and tells us to just go on with our workout. "Don't say anything to anyone," he says. We don't.

Most of the time, Eddie is so drunk that he doesn't even join us on the floor for practice. The assistants run everything. He gets one of the first cellular phones, a big old Motorola pack, and he sits on the sideline talking on that phone and barking out orders to us. Or he calls us over and starts telling us something, and then right in the middle of a sentence falls asleep. Eddie runs the show during games, but there are times in the huddle where he goes off on a tangent or spends the whole time-out chewing out the refs. Sometimes he messes up our names. When it gets to that point, James and Dwane take over.

Coming into mid-January we are still fighting for an SEC title. We follow up that Mississippi State win with one at home over Florida, which improves our record to 9-4. Then we hit our low point, a 76–41 home loss to LSU. We come into the postgame locker room feeling real down. Guys don't say much as they start taking off their uniforms. Eddie walks in and drawls, "Oh no no no, leave that stuff on. We're gonna wait until everybody leaves, and then we're gonna have practice."

That doesn't sound like fun, not least because we haven't eaten since our pregame meal at 2:00 p.m, and I hurled that up hours ago. We sit in the locker room while twenty-four thousand people file out of Rupp Arena. Then we go back onto the floor. Eddie runs us nonstop. At one point, he decides that me and another guy need to run the steps. So we do that for an hour and then come down to rejoin everyone on the court.

When practice ends, he brings us into the film room and shows us video of the game. By this point he is really drunk, and we are really hungry. He starts to go over the film, and he overhears someone talking about how he is starving. "Oh, you're hungry, are you? Hey James, they're hungry," he says, and walks out.

Ten minutes later, Eddie comes back in holding a huge bag of dog food. He rips open the top and pours it all over the floor. "You play like dawgs, you eat like dawgs!" he yells.

Eddie leaves the room, and this time he doesn't come

back. After a couple of minutes, James and Dwane huddle up. Then James says, "All right, guys, go on home. Go get something to eat." He doesn't have to tell us twice.

Next up is a road game at Vanderbilt. We get to the hotel the night before, check into our rooms, and then come back downstairs for dinner. The players and coaches usually sit at different tables. Eddie has gotten there early and is sitting by himself. When he sees us going to our own table, he says to us cheerfully, "What are you all doing? Come on over here."

We look at each other and then do what he says. We can see the guy is hammered but in great spirits. He starts telling us some funny stories. We all egg him on, which is kind of mean. After a while, the assistants come down and see what is going on. James tries to get us to go back to the players' table, but Eddie snaps at him and cracks, "You cut that out." James and Dwane can't do anything, so they take a seat.

Eddie rambles for the next two hours. He is laughing a lot, crying some, talking about his wife and kids one moment, and in the next moment explaining why we should put A.1. Sauce on a potato. It is just random, drunken craziness. Eventually, we finish the meal and go to our rooms.

We end up beating Vanderbilt and follow that up with a pretty good win over eighteenth-ranked Navy, which has David Robinson (who gets a triple-double). From there, we start falling apart. We lose three out of four games and come into the end of February really needing a win against Ole Miss at home. We are down by 1 point with just a few seconds to go, and Eddie calls time-out. He draws up a basic pick-the-picker play to get me the ball. It starts with an in-bounds pass to James Blackmon, who is supposed to hold it until I break clear and then make the pass.

I come off the pick and I am deadass naked wide open at the top of the key. For some reason, James doesn't throw me the ball right away. I scream for it and wave my arms in a panic, and he throws me a slow pass. I manage to catch it a little off-balance, double pump, and launch my shot right before the buzzer. *Swish.* We win, 64–63.

Later that night, the team is having dinner at a restaurant. I am sitting in a booth with James and Ed Davender. James has this grin on his face. He leans in and says, "Y'all don't tell nobody this, but I thought we were up by one."

Ed and I look at each other and bust out laughing. James would have flat dribbled out the clock if he didn't see me frantically ask for the ball.

The next day we play a nationally televised home game against Oklahoma. They are ranked twelfth in the country and have Mookie Blaylock, Harvey Grant, and Stacey King. The following year they will lose to Danny Manning and Kansas in the national championship game. We beat 'em by a point.

Unfortunately, that is our last win of the season. We lose to Auburn in the first round of the SEC tournament and then get destroyed by Ohio State, 91–77, in the NCAA tournament. It is the kind of ending we deserve. The fans are pissed, of course, but they know we have the nation's number one recruiting class coming in, so they give us a pass. That's the good thing about Kentucky basketball. Tomorrow is always a day away.

chapter

7

A few weeks after the season ends, a guy named Eddie Ford, whose son, Travis, will later play for Kentucky, invites me to speak at his basketball camp in Madisonville. On the ride home, he says to me, "I guess you'll have to make a decision here soon." I ask him what he is talking about. "I'm talking about the NBA," he replies. I look at him like he has three heads.

I get away from all the stress for a few days and take a trip with a bunch of my high school buddies to Fort Lauderdale. A wealthy UK booster sends us there on his private plane and lets us stay at his vacation home. The place is magnificent, with a pool out back, a lake in front, cooks living next door who constantly bring us great food. I don't know much about NCAA rules, but I sure know this is illegal. I guess somewhere in my brain I know it's risky, but I never consider not going.

Even after the freshman season I had, I still don't think of myself as an NBA player. As far as I am concerned, I am trying to survive in college. And if I am going to go to the league, it certainly isn't going to be soon.

My mindset changes that summer when I play for Team USA at the Pan Am Games in Indianapolis. I am shocked when Eddie tells me I have been invited to try out. I know that most of the guys on that team are going to be seniors. I am not sure I deserve to be there, but I love the idea of competing. And who is going to be the coach of that team? None other than Denny Crum. I am worried it might be awkward, but Denny makes clear he is gonna treat me fairly.

There are around fifty guys who are invited to the trials in Colorado Springs. There is a good bit of drug use going on in the hotel rooms. Lots of guys are smoking weed, and a few do cocaine. I sit in a room with a couple of guys while they do coke. I don't mind being around it, but I definitely don't want to do it.

This is a familiar story for me. From the time I was thirteen, my buddies in Kentucky smoked weed, but I never tried it. I was afraid I might die, or that I might like it too much. That is especially true with coke. From everything I hear, it sounds like something I would enjoy—and get hooked on. No thanks.

As for alcohol, my mom and dad rarely drank around us. One time when I was young, I asked my dad if I could sip his beer. He said sure and handed me the can. I took a swig and hated it, just as he knew I would. Most of my buddies love to drink, but I have zero interest.

By the time Denny and his staff make the final cuts, I know I am good enough to make the team. But I am shocked when my Kentucky teammate Ed Davender is cut. As far as I'm concerned, he is every bit as good as me, if not better. We were the best backcourt in the country last season. I feel terrible about it, but Ed puts me at ease, which I appreciate. Our training camp is held in Louisville. I room with one of Denny's players, Pervis Ellison. His teammate and my buddy, Kenny Payne, is with us every day during the trials. One day we have some free time, so I go with them to the only mall in Louisville. The second we walk inside, I get mobbed. I don't even notice that Pervis and Kenny have gone into a store. They come out twenty minutes later, and I am still signing autographs. They won the NCAA championship the year before—shit, Pervis was the Most Outstanding Player at the Final Four—and they might as well be invisible. I wish my life was more like theirs.

Denny puts me in the starting lineup. I don't quite realize how good I am, which drives me to work that much harder. I get my basketball education that summer. Every day in practice I play with and against older, really good players, including three future number one overall NBA draft picks in Pervis, Danny Manning, and David Robinson. Yet, I am holding my own and then some. Denny plays me heavy minutes. He doesn't care that I spurned him to play for Louisville's biggest rival. He just wants to win. I truly love that man.

Normally, the Pan Am Games are played outside the States, but that year they are in Indianapolis. We breeze into the gold medal game with an average winning margin of 25 points, so we are pretty complacent heading into the final against Brazil. When we go into the halftime locker room up by 14, it feels like the game is well in hand. In the second half, however, their best player, Oscar Schmidt, starts scoring like crazy. He ends up with 46 points in one of the most legendary performances in the history of international basketball. We lose, 120–115, to break the thirty-four-game US win streak at the Pan Am Games.

In all my life, I had never been and would never be in a locker room where the players were more crushed and shocked. We thought we had the gold wrapped up. Between playing for Denny, bonding with the other players, and doing well in games, that summer is huge for me. I am a lot more confident as a player when I go back to Kentucky for my sophomore season.

● ○ ●

One of the many good things about the start of my sopho-more season is that Reggie can officially join the team. He sat out his freshman season as a non-qualifier, which was really hard for him. I fucking love that dude. We are like the two little kids on the team. Sometimes as we are walking to class, we start skipping in unison. We are goofy like that.

We fuck around with each other all the time. One day, we have a firecracker fight. By "one day," I mean it lasts all day. It will be real quiet for an hour or two, but then I light up a firecracker and fuck him up. Miraculously, we don't set Wildcat Lodge on fire, but we sure make a lot of noise.

It is inevitable that one of us—meaning me—would take things too far. We have this syrup that we use to make sweet tea. Everyone on the team loves it. Our other roommate, Winston Bennett, has to have surgery on his knee, and for a few days he is lying in his bed and pissing in a bedpan. I have been taking the pan and tossing out his piss for him. So right before Reggie comes home one day, I get the idea to pour some of Winston's piss into the syrup and then see if I can get Reggie to drink it.

A few other players come over knowing what is about to go down. Reggie comes home and asks if he can have some of Winston's syrup. "Don't be touching my tea syrup!" Winston yells, playing the gag perfectly.

We sit around eating pizza, trying not to crack up as Reggie pours the syrup into his glass of water. He sips. A confused look comes on his face. We can't hold it in any longer. Reggie is really fucking pissed. He chases me all over the Lodge. It is the only time I know of that he ever gets really mad at me.

A week later, I wake up from one of my long naps and notice that my room smells funny. I don't think much of it, except the smell gets progressively worse over the next couple of days. I can't stand it, but I also can't figure out where it is coming from. Finally, I look under my bed and see a shoebox. I pull it out, open it up, and discover a big pile of shit. I freak out for a second, but I have to admit Reggie got me back pretty good. I find the guy in the building who has the master key, go into Reggie's apartment across the hall, and put the box of shit under his bed. We declare a truce, but it only lasts a little while.

I get him again on the first day of practice. Reggie is so excited about being able to finally play, he wants to get there early. I agree to go with him. Reggie is dealing with a turf toe issue, which can be real problematic for a basketball player. So we go into the trainer's room to get taped. Our trainer, Walt McCombs, is back there with the longtime equipment manager, Bill Keightley. As Walt starts wrapping up Reggie's toe, I say to him, "Hey, Walt, you might have to give him that special tape job and make it a little bigger."

"Oh yeah," Walt says.

Without a smirk or a wink, Walt proceeds to wrap and wrap that toe around until it is huge.

"How am I gonna get my shoe on?" Reggie asks.

"Aww, Reg, you can't wear your regular shoe," I say. I turn to Keightley and say, "Hey Bill, you got Chibby's shoes back there, right?"

Chibby is the nickname of a seven-foot-seven player on the Chinese national team that recently played in Rupp Arena. He wears size 22 shoes, and someone had given Bill a pair as a remembrance. Reggie wears a size 14.

"Sure, no problem, Rex," Bill says. He goes into a back office and brings out one of Chibby's shoes to give to Reggie.

How the three of us get through all of this without cracking up, I don't know, but Reggie buys into it completely. He puts that big old clown shoe on and clops his way onto the court. He takes a few shots while I rebound, while Walt and Bill watch from a tunnel.

Finally, Eddie comes out. He walks over to Reggie to welcome him to his first practice. Eddie looks down at that big clown shoe and says, "Reggie, what are you doin' with that thing?"

I can't take it anymore. I keel over laughing. Here it is, Reggie's first practice, the moment he has been waiting for, and I have just punked him in front of the head coach. He takes off after me and chases me all around the gym. If he weren't wearing one of Chibby's size 22s, he might have caught me.

● ○ ●

While I am spending my summer playing ball for Team USA, Eddie checks himself into the Betty Ford Center in California. You can tell the difference when he gets back to Lexington. He is a lot more clearheaded and engaged—and a lot more mean. At least it seems that way to me, because for the first time he's really coaching me hard. It is like going from a substitute teacher to the real thing.

Those first few weeks of practice are awful. We have two sessions a day of three hours apiece. Eddie wears us out. We have a lot of juniors and seniors on the team. I am the only underclassman who is going to get a lot of minutes. So the senior captains call a players-only meeting to come up with a plan to get Eddie to dial it down. Somehow I get elected to be the team spokesman.

I go into Eddie's office to convey the message. "The players were talking, and we all wondered if maybe you would ease up a little bit," I say. Eddie hears me out but doesn't say much. Before the start of practice, he gathers all of us together. "I just talked to Rex," he says. "I just gotta tell ya, in all my years of basketball, I never had a veteran ball club ask a sophomore to come in and talk to me on behalf of the team." Eddie goes double long that day and just about kills us.

As a freshman, it was almost like I couldn't do anything wrong in Eddie's eyes (on the court, anyway). Now it seems like I can't do anything right. It feels like he is trying to make up for lost time. I resent it, big-time, and I suspect, fairly or not, that a big reason Eddie is acting this way is because he doesn't like that I am so popular with the fans and the media. Sometimes when I'm pissed I think, *I should have gone to Louisville.*

There is a lot of pressure on everyone because, unlike the previous season, we start off with national championship expectations. We are ranked No. 5 in the preseason Associated Press poll, move up to No. 2 the first week, and get to number one after we beat Indiana in overtime at the RCA Dome in Indianapolis on December 5. I notice that Eddie takes shots at me in public but doesn't give me a whole lot of criticism in private. I can tell he's bad-mouthing me to announcers. When we win, everything is great. When we lose, it is all my fault. I feel that I have worked really hard to get to this point. I don't think of myself as a prima donna, although maybe I am becoming one. I want to be coached, but I am also young and still immature in a lot of ways. I feel like he should appreciate me more. Given how he was telling me who I could and could not date made me feel even more resentful.

I'm not the only one having problems with Eddie. Ed Davender is a senior and one of the best guards in the country. Everyone is calling us the best backcourt in the country, but he is losing minutes to Eddie's son Sean, who is a freshman. I like Sean a lot, but the idea that he should be taking minutes from Ed is a fucking joke. In one game, Eddie starts Sean in the second half in Ed's place. Ed is livid, and so am I. After the game, I go to the coaches' locker room to voice my displeasure. The conversation starts to get heated, until James stands up and guides me out of the room.

In my view, Eddie's system is not well suited to the team. We have a bunch of great athletes, but he wants us to walk it up and work the ball around. For a time, there is a seven-pass rule. So Ed and I pass the ball back and forth seven times real quick in the backcourt, and then go play. Eddie hates that.

We win our first ten games, but as the season wears on, things go from bad to worse between me and Eddie. I am convinced he is not standing up for me when I need him to. We talk to each other only when we have to. Other than that, we stay silent and steer clear.

● ○ ●

Jenny enrolls as a freshman that fall. The tension that had built up at home my last couple of years in high school carries over to college, so we don't spend a lot of time together. It seems like there is always a lot of drama with her, and I am having a hard enough time managing my own shit.

I don't spend a whole lot of time with my parents, either. I see them after games, but I rarely go back to Owensboro to visit. As far as I am concerned, when I left that house, I left for good. My relationship with my dad was way better than when I lived at home. I don't tell them about my panic attack or anything else that is going on with me personally. Like everyone else, they just assume everything is going great.

My grandmother is my lifeline. She lives in Lexington, and I go to her place to have some quiet time and drop off my laundry. She cooks for me and Reggie all the time. Being around her makes me feel as close to normal as I can get.

On top of the stress of the season, I am still getting all kinds of shit about my relationship with Shawn. It is a constant source of irritation. I am called in for yet another uncomfortable meeting in Eddie's office. This time, we are joined by a couple of administrative higher-ups in suits. I recognize them because they always sit near the court, though I'm not sure what they do at the school. They sure seem to think they know me, though, because they have a very stern message: You have got to either stop dating Black girls or hide it a lot better. Of course, *they* don't have a problem with it, but some people might, so be cool, right? And it isn't just "some people" but boosters and donors, people who write those big checks that are so important.

It kills me every time I hear this. I know I have to tell

Shawn about it. I want to say to these guys, "You know what? That's a great point. How about we go have this conversation in front of the entire team." But I don't. I sit there like a chickenshit and take in what they have to say. I am glad when the meeting ends and I can go play.

● ○ ●

Our undefeated record finally gets busted on January 9, when we lose at home to Auburn by a point. Two weeks later, we lose by 2 to Florida. We are 13-2 and feeling wobbly when we travel to Vanderbilt in late January. I get into foul trouble and we lose by 16. We win our next five and then drop two straight at Tennessee and Florida, a team we always have trouble with because they have Vernon Maxwell. As a result, we drop out of the top 10 in the national polls, but we know we are good and still have time to get right for the NCAA tournament.

I have bigger problems than trying to beat Florida. Shawn is pregnant. We never used condoms because she was always on the Pill, but I guess she may have missed a few days of taking it. The news is pretty upsetting, but I actually am not freaked out by the idea of having a kid. Whatever Shawn wants, I am fine with it. I tell her that, but she shakes her head. "What are you talking about? We can't have a baby," she says. So she decides to get an abortion. I offer to take her to get the procedure, but she makes the appointment on the same day as our home game against LSU, so she goes without me.

I am playing real well that night until late in the first half, when I get undercut on a dunk attempt and land on my back. I have a difficult time catching my breath. I have to leave the arena and go to the hospital, where an X-ray reveals I have a slight fracture in my lower back. The hospital is a madhouse, with my family, coaches, the media, everybody all over the place, but all I can think about is trying to get ahold of Shawn. It is excruciating. It isn't until late that night, after I get out of the hospital, that I am able to drive over to her place. She had the abortion and is doing okay, all things considered.

Because of that injury, I have to miss our next game, which bums me out because it is at home against Syracuse, which has a star-studded team and is ranked tenth in the country. The guys win without me, which shows just how good we really are. Our next game is at home against Georgia. I do whatever I can to get healthy, including taking Novocain shots, which is about the worst thing you can do in that situation, because if you hurt yourself worse, you can't feel it and don't know it. I put on a back brace and warm up, and I convince the coaches to let me play. We win that game and end the regular season on a four-game win streak. That gives us real momentum heading into the SEC tournament, where we beat Ole Miss and LSU in our first two games and then take down Georgia, 62–57, in the final. I am named MVP.

We are assigned a No. 2 seed in the NCAA tournament and sent to a subregional in Cincinnati. Our first-round game is against Southern, which has a real good point guard in Avery Johnson. Southern plays in the SWAC and loves to get up and down. We win, 99–84. It is the first time all season we are able to play racehorse basketball, and we love it. We beat Maryland by 9 in the second round to move on to the Sweet 16 against Villanova.

That's where it all ends. I have a career-high 30 points, but Villanova goes on a 14–3 run late in the first half, and we never recover. Villanova makes just about every free throw down the stretch, and they upset us, 80–74.

I averaged 25.3 points per game in the three NCAA tournament games, and I made 52.6 percent from three-point range. But the bottom line is we lost. I am still in a state of shock after the game when I am sitting at my locker and talking to reporters. Ralph Hacker, who is one of our main radio broadcasters, asks me a question about my plans for next year. I am in such a haze, I can't even think straight. I brush him off by saying something like "I don't know what's gonna happen next season" and figure that is that.

By the time we get back to Lexington that night, my comment has become a huge story. People are panicking that I am going to enter the NBA draft instead of coming back for my junior season. That was truly not my intent when I said those words. But I guess subconsciously I knew what I was doing, because I am not ready to commit to coming back for my junior season. Enough people have told me that the NBA is a possibility that I feel I at least have to look into it. Between my frayed relationship with Eddie and all the shit I've been getting about dating Shawn, the idea of leaving Kentucky is becoming more and more appealing.

When I get back to my room that night, Dwane calls and

asks if I will come meet with the coaches at the Coliseum the next day. They ask what my plans are, and I tell them I honestly don't know. Over the next few days, I get very serious about the possibility of leaving for the NBA. The NBA doesn't have a predraft combine like they will years later, and I don't work out for a bunch of teams. I lean on my dad, who speaks to some NBA guys he knows, including Jerry West. I go to see Dan Issel, the former Kentucky great, who has just retired from the NBA and is living in the state. All the people we talk to basically tell me the same thing. There are some aspects of my game that need to get better, but I have shown enough potential that if I do enter the draft, I'll get picked high.

Once that becomes clear, it makes my decision easy. I let Eddie and the coaches know what I have decided, but they ask if I will wait a few days before making an official announcement. A couple hours later, Eddie sets up a meeting with some boosters in his office. The boosters tell me that with where I am projected to get drafted, I will make about $700,000 in salary my first year. "If you stay," they say, "we'll make it work for you."

I can't believe it. The same people who've tried to tell me who I can and can't date are willing to do whatever it takes to get me to spend one more season in Lexington. These guys think they are making me want to stay, when in truth they are only confirming for me that leaving is the right thing to do.

While I'm figuring out what to do, the *Daily News* of Los Angeles breaks a huge story regarding an Emery envelope addressed from Dwane Casey to Chris Mills, a prominent recruit who lived in LA, that had "accidentally" opened and revealed $1,000 in cash inside. It's clear that a major scandal is coming, and I definitely don't want to stick around to see how it plays out, especially since I know full well how this program operates. One year later, Eddie and the entire coaching staff will be forced to resign, but Dwane always denies that he sent that cash. I never believe for one second that Dwane sent that envelope. He is way too smart for that. I'm later proven right when Dwane sues Emery and settles the case for what was reported to be a seven-figure amount. The NCAA will end up lifting its ban on Dwane when he's able to show he never did anything wrong.

I go home to Owensboro to finalize my decision. I think I might want to transfer to Louisville. I would love to play for Denny there, but the NCAA has a rule—which would later be changed—that if you transfer, you have to sit out a year before playing again. There is no way I am gonna do that. So really, if I want to leave Kentucky, there is nowhere for me to go but the NBA.

I don't even bother holding a press conference. I release the news to someone in the local media and file my paperwork with the league. Just like that, my college career is over.

● ○ ●

I still have to finish out the semester at UK, so I drive back to school. I pull up to Wildcat Lodge and find Reggie on the front steps. He is damn near tears. All my shit is sitting in a pile in the parking lot. Apparently, the coaches sent over a couple of managers to move my belongings out of my room. I might be a student at Kentucky technically, but I am no longer a member of the team, which they say means I am not allowed to live in the Lodge anymore. *Fuck 'em.* I split time between my grandmother's house and Shawn's apartment, and I finish out the school year.

Later in life, I will still get a lot of love from Kentucky fans, and I really appreciate it, but I'll always feel that there's a part of the fan base that has never forgiven me for leaving early. I also believe that's a big reason why my jersey has never been retired. After I am done playing in the NBA, someone high up in the athletic department tells me that the school will "consider" retiring my jersey if I will "consider" donating $50,000. "You can retire my jersey if you want," I tell him. "But I'm damn sure not paying for it."

chapter

8

After I enter the draft, I meet with several agents and decide to hire David Falk. David represents all the top players in the league, including Michael Jordan, so he has a ton of leverage with the teams. We click right away.

My next big decision is whether to try out for the 1988 Summer Olympics coached by John Thompson of Georgetown. This will turn out to be the last Olympic team made up only of college players. David warns me that it could hurt my draft status, but I don't care. I feel like it is a once-in-a-lifetime opportunity, and there is no doubt in my mind I will play well.

Unfortunately, I have a really bad hip pointer that bothers me throughout the trials. I go with the team on an exhibition tour in Europe and play pretty well considering I am hurt. Sean Elliott and I are the last two players cut. It is the first time in my life I am told that I'm not good enough to make a team.

The NBA invites me to come to the draft in New York, which is a good indication I am going to be picked pretty high. Draft night is a very nerve-racking experience. David thinks I'm going to get picked sixth by the Clippers, but they end up choosing Hersey Hawkins of Bradley. I don't care where I go, but the waiting is torture. After the seventh pick, David tells me I am going to the Charlotte Hornets, which is an expansion team about to play its first season. I hadn't even visited them, but by this point, I just want to get it over with. When my name is called, I feel relief more than elation.

The next day, I fly to Charlotte to meet with the local media. David lets me know that it could be a little while before my contract gets finalized. Rookies' salaries aren't predetermined like they would be years later. While David and the team hammer out the details, I go back to Kentucky to hang with my friends and work out.

There is this really cool, modern apartment complex in Lexington next to Rupp Arena called Centre City Condos. The owners think that having me stay there is good for business, so they give me the penthouse. Big mistake. I am only twenty years old and have a bunch of close friends who are still in college. That penthouse is one big, nonstop party.

One night we have a bunch of people over, and there is partying going on throughout the building. Some frat guys are there. They tell me they have some mushrooms. I have no idea what they are talking about. They explain that these are psychedelic mushrooms that grow out of cow shit. Now *that* sounds appetizing. But they make it seem like fun, and unlike cocaine, it is a natural drug that grows out of the earth. I don't know why, but I say, sure, count me in.

The mushrooms taste as awful as I thought they would. As I am eating them, my friends warn me, "This is gonna be like being on a team. The number one rule is, don't leave your teammates. When you're at the party, you can lock eyes with one of us, and we'll know we're on the same team."

I don't feel anything at first. A girl shows up that I invited to the party, and I start hanging with her. I am feeling tingly about an hour later when another girl I had mistakenly invited shows up, too. Uh-oh. I am trying to figure out how I am going to navigate the situation and offer to go get her a beer. I get the beer and start pouring the drink . . . right onto the ground. The mushrooms have fully kicked in.

My friends take me into another room and we sit for a long time. Or it might only be a few minutes. Time doesn't mean much when you're shrooming. I feel like the clock has said 11:37 for an hour. I am laughing harder than I ever have in my life. Just weird psychedelic shit. At one point, someone in the room starts throwing up on the floor. I feel like it is raining.

Next thing I know, I am alone. My mood does a complete 180. I start freaking, thinking I am gonna die. There are people in the room next door blasting heavy metal music, which makes it worse. I am thinking how disappointed my mom and dad will be that their son has died of a drug overdose right after getting drafted by the NBA.

I manage to walk out of the room. I have ripped my shirt and look ridiculous. In time, the mushrooms wear off. The experience is scary, but those guys did me a big favor. I already had an aversion to drugs. Now I know for sure they are not for me.

● ○ ●

The hardest part of waiting for my contract to get done is finding a high-quality game to stay sharp. I go to Owensboro for a while and run with my dad's players, but that isn't going to be enough. When I mention my dilemma to David, he asks if I want to spend a few weeks with Michael Jordan in Chapel Hill.

Aside from that phone call when North Carolina was trying to recruit me, I don't know Michael real well. He welcomes me to Chapel Hill, and we work out a lot. It is very generous of him, but I also get the sense he is sizing me up, knowing he is going to play against me. He is always looking for a competitive edge.

The first morning I am there, we have a 7:00 a.m. tee time. By the time I get up, Michael has already gone for a six-mile run. He walks back in the house in a full lather. It is the only time he does that during the week I am with him.

We spend the week training. We compete just as hard at golf and cards. That also means drinking, cigars, and gambling. I'm not a drinker or smoker, but I am happy to join in on the gambling. We play basketball for a couple of hours and then play golf all day. On some days, we get in sixty holes.

One day a few older guys join us. We set up a match, but I don't realize how much money we are playing for. You'd think I'd want to know that since I have exactly zero dollars to my name. At the end of my visit, I find out I owe one of the other guys ten grand. No problem, I say, and write a check. Then I call a booster at Kentucky and ask him to wire me fifty grand so I can cover my losses.

The closer we get to training camp, the more nervous I get that my contract isn't done. The Hornets are offering me a $650,000 salary. David is asking for $675,000. He tells me to hold out for a little longer and refuse to report to camp in order to get the team to move our way.

We fly to Charlotte and try to close out the deal at the house of the team's owner, George Shinn. While David is upstairs hammering out the deal with the CFO, George and I hang out in his basement. George has a bar set up downstairs, but I don't drink alcohol, so he pours me a Coke. We are talking about nothing much, and then George abruptly pivots the conversation. "Do you have a Black girlfriend?" he asks.

An all-too-familiar feeling hits my gut. "No," I say, which is true because Shawn and I are broken up at the time. "But if I did and that makes me a bad guy, then I guess I'm a bad guy."

He seems to be surprised by my defensive tone. "Yeah, yeah, of course," he says. "I'm just saying you need to be careful with stuff like that. Remember, we live in the Bible Belt."

The Bible Belt. I have never heard that term before, but I recognize the tired, twisted logic. Of *course*, George has no objections to interracial dating, but, well, *other* people won't like it, people who read the *Bible,* so you know, be careful, kid. It is completely deflating. I honestly thought I had left that ignorant shit behind in college.

This is the first time I have ever stuck up for myself on this issue. My reaction to his question appears to have rattled him, because a short while later George goes upstairs and tells the CFO to pay me the $675,000. For most of my NBA career, the running joke in the locker rooms for all the former Kentucky players will be "You took a pay cut to go to the NBA." Turns out that was actually true in my case.

There is no way I know how to get myself a place to live, so I hire a lady in Lexington to do all that for me. She finds me a two-bedroom, two-floor unit in an apartment complex and furnishes it. I get there, unpack my stuff, and take in my new surroundings.

I have never lived on my own before. The first night I am in the living room watching TV late and I decide it is time to go to bed. So I shut off the TV, start walking upstairs . . . and I just stop. It is totally dark on the top floor. I think, *Screw it,* go back downstairs, and fall asleep with the TV on. Here I am, a twenty-year-old NBA lottery pick, and I am still afraid of the dark.

● ○ ●

The first friends I make in Charlotte are Dell Curry and his wife, Sonya. They live in the same complex, and they happen to be standing outside when I first pull up. Dell is a shooting guard, so he and I are going to compete for minutes, but he couldn't be nicer.

Sonya is great to me, too, even though I date one of her cousins. She helps me with my laundry—or should I say, does it for me, because I have no idea how. One time we go on a long road trip, and since I don't know how to do laundry I buy like sixty pairs of underwear. When we get home, Sonya comes over, and she busts out laughing when she sees all those unopened packets.

Dell mentors me in so many ways. We have a team function early in the season where we all have to wear suits. I have no idea how to tie a tie. When I tell Dell, he just smiles and shakes his head. Then we go to a mirror, and Dell stands behind me and teaches me how to tie a tie like he is my dad.

My other best friend on the team is our point guard, Tyrone "Muggsy" Bogues, who also lives in the apartment complex with his wife, Kim, and their baby girl, Brittney. There had never been and will never be a player in the NBA like Muggsy. He is five foot three, which should have disqualified him from playing high school ball, much less the NBA, but he was a star at Wake Forest and was picked twelfth overall in the 1987 draft by the Washington Bullets, who then traded him to Charlotte at the end of his rookie season.

Dell and Sonya have one baby. His name is Stephen. I haven't been around babies a whole lot, but I love being with Stephen. If Dell and Sonya want to go out to dinner, they ask me to babysit. I change his diapers and everything. Otherwise,

Dell takes Stephen everywhere. Dell, Muggsy, and I will be riding in the car, thinking we are great players. Little do we know the best player in the car is sitting in the baby seat.

One time we are riding around, and Stephen is making a huge racket. I am back there next to him, and Dell suggests I take him out of the seat to see if I can get him to stop crying. I guess Stephen is tired, because as soon as his head hits my chest, he is out. I try not to move because I don't want to wake him up and have to listen to that crying again. I feel Stephen's heart beating against my chest. I know then and there that someday I am gonna be a dad.

● ○ ●

I am just a dumbass rookie—I have four cars, for fuck's sake—but those guys tolerate me. My calves are so big, I have to get special zippers sewed into my jeans. Nobody knows but Dell and Muggsy. They tease me about it mercilessly. We are riding the bus one night during the preseason to play the Bulls. Dell and Muggsy aren't gonna play, so I am gonna get a lot of minutes at shooting guard. Someone on the bus says to me, "You got Michael tonight." I shoot back, "You mean Michael's got *me*."

Dell rolls his eyes and says to Muggsy, "He's about to get baptized by Black Jesus." I see what they mean when the game begins. I realize right away that this guy is just different.

Dell fractured his right wrist a few months ago, and he is still wearing a cast on his shooting hand when training camp began. Even after the cast comes off, it takes a while for him to get back into game shape. Not only is Dell one of the best shooters in the history of the league, he is older than me and a lot smarter. Because he is unavailable the first few weeks, our coach, Dick Harter, plays me more minutes than I deserve.

I am by far the youngest guy on the team—I am actually the youngest player in the league—but I always feel comfortable in the locker room. I have national sponsorship deals with Wendy's and Coke, and the team is promoting the shit out of me, but I never feel any resentment from the other players. The only other rookie is Tom Tolbert, but he is still a couple years older than me. Most of the other guys are college graduates and married with kids. We go out for drinks sometimes as a group, and a few of them smoke weed. They are all really good to me, but aside from Muggsy and Dell, I don't have much in common with my teammates outside of playing.

I knew I'd have a lot of adjusting to do, but reality sets in those first few weeks of the regular season. This is the first time in my life I am on a team where I'm not the best shooter. It is also the first time I get open shots, because defenses are more concerned with guarding my teammates sometimes. Logically, it should be easier to shoot when you're open, but when it's something you're not used to, it is difficult. On top of all that, my back starts acting up again. I strained a muscle and overcompensated, which only makes the pain worse. The team puts me on injured reserve, which means I have to sit for five games. It sucks having to go to the chiropractor and physical therapy every day, but it is incredibly valuable for me to watch all those games from the sideline. I can study not only my teammates but guys on other teams like Reggie Miller and Ron Harper without having to worry about guarding them.

My first chance to come back is for a game against the Bulls. Someone asks me if I am sure I want my first game back to be against Michael, but I insist. It never occurs to me not to play. My dad comes to that game, and afterward he tells me he's never been prouder of me because I was so eager to compete against the best even after the long layoff. Coming from a guy who almost never complimented me about how I played, that means a lot.

● ○ ●

Eventually, I am able to settle down and play without trying to go a million miles an hour all the time. Kurt Rambis is one of the first people to teach me to be conscientious about scouting reports. He is getting old and is all banged up. When I asked him in training camp how long he planned to play, he said, "Until every team in the league rips the jersey off my back."

We have a battle going on with the league's other expansion franchise, the Miami Heat, not to have the worst record in the league. We both know where the other is in the standings. On the nights we play them, that is our NBA Finals. We play hard against other teams, too, but it doesn't usually matter. We'll stay close for the first three quarters, then they'll turn it on in the fourth and beat us.

I have never lost like this in my life, and it crushes me. One night Rickey Green, who has been in the league for ten years, sits next to me and tries to put it all in perspective. "Look, we're gonna lose three out of every four games," he says. "That's just the way it is. You need to get up fifteen shots a night, win or lose."

I don't know what I would do without Muggsy and Dell. Muggsy is one of the funniest people I have ever met—intentionally and unintentionally. That little fucker can *go*. He is so fast and clever, and he loves nothing more than getting buckets for his teammates. He gets really pissed if he gives you a great pass and you miss the shot. "Rex, you fucked up my dime, man!" he'll say. Or if I catch the ball and try to drive, he'll say, "Why'd you dribble? I gave it to you so you didn't have to dribble."

He is so fast on the break that nobody can keep up with him. He directs traffic by putting his finger behind his back and pointing where we should run. He is maybe the smartest player I've ever played with. Sometimes Dick will draw up a play in the huddle. Then when we walk on the court, Muggsy will grab me and say, "Nah nah nah, this is what we're gonna do."

Muggsy loves playing defense, too. No matter who he is being assigned to guard that night, he'll look at us and say, "Oh, he's got a high dribble." Everyone says he had to overcome his height, but he thinks of it as an advantage. Muggsy will bait his guy by letting him dribble a few times, then he'll be on that ball as soon as it hits the ground. Or he'll tell us to let our guy drive to the baseline and then turn him back to the middle. When he does, Muggsy has it timed perfectly so that as soon as the guy dribbles, he is right there for the steal.

Of course, everyone tries to post him up. That is fine with us, because if they're throwing it in the post to their point guard, that means they aren't throwing it to their center. And heaven forbid you try to double-team the guy as he is backing Muggsy down. Muggsy will get pissed and shout, "I got him!" He knows they are trying to bully him, and he wants to handle it himself.

Muggsy and I come from very different backgrounds, but we immediately become best friends. That's the beauty of team sports. He grew up in a real rough part of Baltimore. When he was five years old, a neighbor pulled out a rifle to scare off some kids who were messing with his property. Muggsy was standing nearby and got hit with some buckshot and had to go to the hospital. Another time he saw a neighbor damn near beat a man to death with a baseball bat. His dad spent thirteen years in prison.

The fans really love Muggsy. He smiles and is completely approachable. I learn so much from him about how to handle all that. He signs autographs, poses for pictures, and chats with people. The only thing that pisses him off is if a grown-up puts their hand on his head. "I ain't no mother-fucking kid," he'll say.

I have my share of good moments that rookie season. My tenth game is on the road against the Celtics. Boston Garden has a great floor for jumping. I get a breakaway and take off for the rim. I think I jumped too early, but I get there and flush it. I score 21 that night, and for the first time feel like if I buckle down, I can be a good player in this league.

Later in the season, we are playing at Atlanta, and I track down Reggie Theus on a fast break and swat his shot into the stands. That feels amazing. I average 16.9 points per game, which is second-highest on the team, but I only shoot 31.4 percent from three-point range. Athletically, I can keep up, but I have very little understanding of how to play the NBA game. Maybe I am more athletic than a guy like Rolando Blackman, but he has a lot more experience than I do. He is a *way* better shooter, and he knows all the tricks. I have a lot to learn, but I know it, and I am willing to work as hard as necessary to get better.

We only win twenty games that season, but at least it is five more than the Heat. Yet, the fans in Charlotte love us. We have twenty-four thousand at every game, and they are loud. We want to win for them and feel badly when we don't. As bad as we are, we actually lead the league in attendance, which the team commemorates with a banner. Hey, at least we are good at something.

chapter

9

The idea of spending my summers in Charlotte by myself is highly unappealing, so I buy a condo in Lexington and stay there for most of the off-season. It is right next to a unit that is owned by another former Kentucky player, Kenny Walker. He and I were already tight, but spending those summers together brings us closer. Our balconies are side by side, and we each have a hot tub.

Kentucky has just hired a new coach in Rick Pitino, and he invites Kenny and me to be around his players whenever we want. We take full advantage. Running, lifting, swimming, playing, working out—whatever they do, we do. It is great for us, but Rick knows it will be good for his players as well. The program is in rough shape because of all the NCAA penalties, but it is obviously only a matter of time before Rick will get things going again.

It is a strange existence. I'm a twenty-one-year-old college dropout from Owensboro. For the first time in my life I have real money, and I have no idea how to handle it. I don't have a single notion about investing or buying stock or any of that shit. I have people working for me who watch my money and pay my bills. I don't write checks because I don't know how to balance a checkbook—and don't have to learn. In my mind, none of it matters. As long as I am not falling into drinking and drugs, I am able to convince myself that I am doing great.

I have lots of money and downtime and very few hobbies. Bad combination. I buy a new car every six months or so. My real downfall is the racetrack. The more money I make playing ball, the more I bet, which is usually how these things go.

When summer ends, I go back to Charlotte for my second season in the NBA. I pick up Dell at his place so we can go to the first practice. Before we get to the car, Stephen runs out of the apartment and yells, "Daddy!" I didn't even know he had learned to talk. I can't believe one of my best friends has a kid who is calling him "Daddy." From then on, that's what I call Dell.

Stephen wants to be everywhere Dell is. Whenever Dell explains that he has to leave, Stephen whines, "You gotta go to practice *again*?" When Stephen gets a little older, he loves hanging out in the locker room with us. He'll be off to the side shooting wads of paper into a garbage can. During our games, he'll be in a back room set up for the players' kids, and they get all sweaty and breathless playing on a Nerf hoop.

David Thompson, the legendary NC State star, still lives in the area and works for the Hornets as an ambassador. I worshipped David when I was growing up. His NBA career was cut short because of knee issues, but he plays one-on-one with me and kicks my ass. After he plays a few times, he has to wait a couple of weeks because his knees swell up. It is a thrill to be out there with one of my childhood heroes.

Year two in Charlotte has a different wrinkle in that we have switched to the Western Conference. The league decided to flip-flop us with the Heat. As the season gets going, I can feel my hard work start to pay off. Before I got to the NBA, I don't think I ever attempted a shot fake. Now I am learning all the little tricks of the game. I also get to the foul line a lot more. As a result, all my numbers go up across the board.

Still, there is no denying how young I am. Whenever I have a good game, someone will invariably say, "And he'd only be a senior at Kentucky." That doesn't help me with the folks back home, considering the Cats are really struggling. Kentucky fans refer to Rick's first team as "The Young and the Rexless."

NBA players want to kill each other on the court, but there is a genuine respect and affection that I feel right away. Between playing on the road, hanging out in bars and clubs, and attending various functions, I feel like the older vets are looking out for me. Magic Johnson and Isiah Thomas are sponsored by Converse, too, so we are around each other quite a bit. I idolized Isiah growing up. When I was in eighth grade I wore his number and Adidas shoes. Now he's my friend, which is super cool and a little weird. Other guys go out of their way to be nice as well, even though we are technically competitors. As I get older, I will always try to extend that same courtesy for the younger guys coming in.

My parents come down to Charlotte a bunch and go to the games. They often sit with Dell's parents. Dell is real close with his family, especially his dad, who calls Dell before every game. One night we are in Los Angeles, and we are eating in Dell's room. The phone rings, and Dell answers. He drops his head as he listens. When the call is over, Dell starts sobbing and throwing things around the room. I can't tell what he is saying at first, but it is soon apparent that his dad has died of a heart attack. He was only fifty-eight years old. Dell calls Muggsy, too, and the two of us do what we can to support him, but he is inconsolable. I don't want to play the game that night, but Dell insists.

Michael Jordan's parents still live in the area, and they come to a lot of the games. Michael is becoming a good friend, largely because of our mutual relationship with David Falk. The most underrated aspect of Michael's game is his hands. They are strong and absolutely enormous. One time we are playing in Chicago, and I go to a bowling alley the night before the game to hang with Michael and some of our friends. At one point, one of the pins gets stuck in the gutter. While we are looking around to find someone who can help, Michael reaches toward the rack, palms a ball with one hand, and backhands it down the lane like it is a tennis ball.

I look around in shock, but the guys who are with us aren't surprised.

Having hands like that makes basketball a different game for Michael. He can grab the ball in midair with one hand and change directions. His mind is even quicker than his body. There are several times I shot fake and drive by him. Against 99 percent of NBA players, that move leads to a dunk, but Michael can recover and foul me or swipe the ball away before I go into my move. If you do beat Michael, he tries to foul you hard. He never, ever gives up on a play. He has a deep competitiveness that other mortals do not have. I'm just breaking into this league, and I know I have a long way to go to be as good as Michael Jordan, but slowly, and surely, I am proving I belong.

● ○ ●

When it comes to the opposite sex, the NBA is an extension of college. If we have a road game, there are women waiting for us at the hotel. If there aren't, it isn't hard at all to go out somewhere, meet a woman, and bring her back to your room.

For most of my first three years in the NBA, I am still seeing Shawn. We spend time together when I am back in Lexington. I take her to a Stevie Wonder concert at Rupp Arena. We get great tickets, and when the show is over, someone comes over to us and asks if we want to meet Stevie. Of course we say yes.

They take us backstage, and after a while Stevie comes out to say hello. "This is Rex Chapman," his friend says. "He played basketball for Kentucky."

"Hey, Rex," Stevie cracks. "I've seen you play!"

Shawn flies to Charlotte a few times to visit. She usually sits with Sonya Curry at the games. Lots of people know we are together, and I figure some of them aren't happy about it. A part of me likes upsetting people who are racist assholes.

I wish I could just do what I want to do and not have to worry about that kind of stupid shit. We play a game at Indianapolis and I see Detlef Schrempf, the Pacers' talented young forward from Germany, hanging out in a hallway after the game with his Black girlfriend. I am jealous as hell. I thought that wasn't something I was allowed to do, when in truth I don't have the balls to be who I want to be.

One time, a girl from my past calls to tell me that she has a child and I am the father. I do the math in my head and figure she could be right, but I hope it isn't true. I have always tried to be careful by using protection, but she was on the Pill, so I didn't with her. The situation sends me into a near panic until her sister calls and assures me the baby is not mine. She sends me a picture, which makes me exhale. The kid is half Chinese.

There is another time when my teammates let me know that there is a woman who sits regularly behind our bench at home games who seems to be taking a particular interest in me. I don't know much about her except she is the wife of a local financial guy. I'd guess she is about twenty years older than me. I don't think much of it at first, but once in a while I glance over at her, and I see what the guys are talking about. It is spooky.

One night I am leaving the arena, and this fancy car pulls up right next to me. It is her. She waves at me and drives away. I get into my car, start driving home, and I realize she is following me. She tails me all the way to my subdivision. When I pull into my driveway, she drives away.

This happens several more times. Now I start to really panic. I tell Muggsy and Dell what is going on. They give me a ton of shit and zero help. Then one night I look out my window and see a car parked outside my apartment. I'm not sure if it is her, but it is definitely suspicious. After this happens a couple of times, I finally decide I am going to go out there and see what is up. When I do, the car peels off.

My teammates tell me that the next time I see her near my home, I should call the police. That's what I do. When the police show up, the car tries to drive off, but the cops trap it in the parking lot. Sure enough, it is my stalker. They find her completely naked in the front seat along with a bunch of sex toys. I am standing about thirty feet away when they start to question her, and then I slip back inside my apartment and let them handle it. I'm not sure what happens from there or whether her husband ever finds out, but it is a long while before I see her at a game again.

● ○ ●

I have a terrific first half of the season, but I am looking forward to a few days off at the All-Star break. Then the Hornets and the NBA basically tell me I need to be in the slam dunk contest. I turned down the invitation as a rookie, but this time

I feel obligated to say yes. Also, my UK buddy Kenny Walker is doing it, so I figure it will be fun. The game and the contest are in Miami that year. Dominique Wilkins wins it—of course—but I more than hold my own. I give no thought to the fact that I am the only white guy in the contest. I know I belong, and that is enough for me. Later in life, I'll get pissed when people try to say I was one of the best white dunkers of all time. Fuck that, I was a great dunker, Black *or* white. Don't put me in that box, man.

My being white and the way I play comes up from time to time in the locker room, but it is always good-naturedly. During my rookie year, we were playing in Milwaukee, and I was assigned to guard Ricky Pierce. I didn't know much about him, but he was older, smarter, bigger, and stronger than I was, and he absolutely kicked my ass. At one point, he went into the post three straight possessions and scored on me with ease. After the last bucket, he ran by our bench and shouted, "You better get this white motherfucker off me!"

I wasn't insulted in the least. Fuck, I just about *agreed* with him.

● ○ ●

Toward the end of my second season in Charlotte, my dad decides to retire. He had won two Division II national championships at Kentucky Wesleyan, but the school is financially struggling, and he has been passed over for some bigger opportunities. Plus, he has a son who is making NBA money. He is only forty-four years old, but he walks away from coaching and never goes back.

I have already been giving my parents a few grand a month and bought them a house in Lexington, and I am glad to help them out. But now things become more formal, as my father starts working for me in real estate and other businesses. We decide to open up a restaurant in Lexington. It is called 3's, and it is pretty popular for a while, but he is an inexperienced businessman, and the bar will go belly-up after a few years. So we buy some low-income apartments and decide he will manage them for me.

When your parents become financially dependent on you, it alters the relationship. Unfortunately, my dad ends up spending way too much time and money at Keeneland racetrack. I find out because we have an issue with the bank. He has to come clean and gets very emotional about it. He feels horribly guilty, and I am shocked.

Things also get real bad between me and my sister. I would come home during the off-season, and Jenny seems to expect me to do stuff for her and buy her things. She calls from time to time when she needs a new laundry machine and stuff like that. It begins to feel like the only time I hear from Jenny is when she needs money. One time I buy her a brand-new Trans Am, but she doesn't know she is supposed to change the oil. She drives that thing until the engine falls out.

I play well during the second half of the season, but in early March I develop a sharp pain in my shin. I try pushing through, but it gets so bad that I have to take myself out of a home game against Detroit. The team doctor takes some X-rays that reveal stress fractures in a tibia and fibula. I am done for the season.

Despite that setback, there are plenty of reasons to believe that my career is on a good trajectory. And yet, I still am not happy. All my life I have dreamt of playing in the NBA, and now that it has come true, I am stuck wondering, *Is this all there is?* My two-faced existence continues. Things are going royally on the basketball court, but when I am away from the game, I can't get outside my own head. And I don't know what to do about it.

chapter
10

I go back to Lexington again for the summer. I am out at a bar one night with my buddies when I run into a girl named Bridget Hobbs. She grew up in Hardinsburg, a small town of about twenty-five hundred people not far from Owensboro. Her dad, Dean, was the basketball coach at Breckinridge County High School. He was the opposing coach in the game where I broke the kid's nose. Bridget went to UK, but we didn't hang out a whole lot. I am glad to see her. I ask if she wants to go out in the next couple of days, and she says yes. Driving home in my Ferrari, I get pulled over by a cop for driving too slowly. When the officer discovers I have a suspended license, he arrests me. I spend a couple of hours in a Georgetown jail while it all gets sorted out. The news never leaks, thankfully.

As a result, I totally forget about my date with Bridget.

It's not until I'm back in Charlotte a few months later that I remember. I call her right away. She tells me to fuck off and hangs up on me, which is exactly what I deserve.

I don't average as many points during my third season with the Hornets, but my field goal percentage goes way up to 44.5. I go to the free-throw line more than ever and knock down 83 percent. I play in seventy of our eighty-two games (up from fifty-four the year before) and start sixty-eight of them. I participate in the slam dunk contest again at the All-Star break and come in third. That is the contest where Dee Brown of the Boston Celtics leans down and pumps his Reebok shoes before taking off. The Hornets win only twenty-six games and finish last again in the Atlantic Division, but I finally feel like a legit, high-level NBA player.

I go back to Lexington for the summer of 1991 excited about taking the next step—and having some fun, of course. Kenny Walker and I resume our workouts with the Wildcats, while I indulge in my usual passions: golf, cars, horses, women. Something has changed in me, though. I sign a five-year contract extension with the Hornets for $10 million. That sounds like $10 billion to me. I think I can spend that money any way I want and it will last me forever. For some reason I have it in my mind that I need to get married. I go on a few dates with a girl I hung out with when I was at Kentucky. We go to lunch one day at a Friday's restaurant in Louisville. "What would you say if I asked you to marry me?" I say.

She scoffs and replies, "That's not how you ask someone,

Rex." I am pissed because I wasn't really trying to propose to her, but she's acting like I did.

I learn later on that Rick Pitino and his wife, Joanne, have just hired a math tutor for their kids. It's Bridget Hobbs, the girl from Kentucky who I blew off the previous summer. When Bridget starts working for Rick, it gives us a chance to reconnect. Pretty soon we are spending a lot of time together. Later that summer, I fly out to LA to play in Magic Johnson's charity game. Bridget comes with me, and I dare her to fly with me to Vegas the next day so we can get married. We make the trip, but she backs out.

When Bridget asks Rick what he thinks about us getting married, he says, "Don't do it." He thinks it is a terrible idea for anyone to marry an athlete. When I ask his opinion, he says, "If you're gonna do this, sign a prenup." Neither of us take his advice. We get engaged shortly after we get back to Lexington.

The toughest part of the whole experience is telling Shawn. She is dumbfounded. She knows Bridget a little because they had cheered against each other in high school, but she didn't even know we were dating, much less talking about getting married. I tell myself that it isn't my fault, that I never promised Shawn anything. But I absolutely break her heart, and I never forgive myself for that.

The idea of holding a big wedding in Kentucky turns my stomach. It will be a big spectacle and a huge hassle. So we decide to plan a small destination wedding in the Bahamas. Things are moving real fast, but it isn't fast enough, because while all the planning is going on, Bridget and I get the bright idea to elope to Vegas. We fly there, get married at the Little White Wedding Chapel, and go home the next day. *No one knows about it.*

A month later, a small group of family and close friends fly to the Bahamas for the wedding. I have my bachelor party the night before. My buddies take me to a strip club, and Bridget and her girlfriends surprise us and show up. It is hell trying to get everyone out of bed the next morning to go to the airport. We make the flight—barely—but Bridget is pissed off for a couple of days. Meanwhile, the whole time, we are already married. It is a big ruse. We go through with the ceremony and everything. It is about ten years before we tell any of our family and friends what we did.

● ○ ●

Dell and Muggsy can't believe it when I tell them the news. They are so shocked, they aren't even mad that I hadn't invited them to the wedding. I'm not sure what surprises them more: that I had gotten married so quickly or that my wife is white. Either way, it is going to be a major adjustment for me, and I will have to manage my new reality without letting it affect my performance on the court.

With everything going on in my personal life, my training is nowhere near what it needs to be—and it shows. When you're out of shape, you're just begging to get injured, so right away I pull my hamstring in training camp. Then I try to come back too soon, which is another mistake, because if you are playing hurt, you compensate in other areas of your body, and the problem snowballs. I eventually develop plantar fasciitis in my foot. I try to play through the pain by taking Novocain shots, but the team shuts me down in early December.

This whole time, Bridget has been working back in Lexington as an elementary school teacher. She comes and visits me on weekends. Even though we are married, we are still getting to know each other. I get the sense that we aren't clicking, but I have no frame of reference because I don't know what marriage is supposed to be like. The thing I am realizing most is that Bridget and I are two very different people. I like to be silly and laugh all the time, and she is just the opposite. She is also a much bigger planner than I am—but then again, so are most people.

I notice how welcoming everyone is to Bridget, especially back home, even though they barely know her. They sure didn't extend that same courtesy to Shawn, whom they all knew well. This only adds to my resentment.

Our original plan was for Bridget to finish out the school year and then move in with me permanently. That is, until she tells me she is pregnant. As usual, it is a huge life decision that I didn't plan for, but I am happy about it. We decide then that she will quit teaching and live full-time in Charlotte.

In February, I find out that I am being traded to the Washington Bullets. That is a really weird feeling. It is the first time in my life I am on a team that doesn't want me. Bridget and I move to DC as quickly as we can so I can continue my rehab for my foot. I get myself well enough that I am able to play in the final regular season game at Philadelphia. I have 10 points in 22 minutes and miss both three-pointers I take. I am glad to be back in a game, but I have a long off-season ahead. I am determined to make the most of my fresh start.

● ○ ●

The Bullets pick up my contract when they acquire me. I have all the usual outlets, but none interest me more than horse racing. I was lucky there were no racetracks in Charlotte. If I have some time on the road and there is a track nearby, I head over there and spend the day.

Once Off Track Betting comes along, I am all in. I know where every OTB is in every NBA city. These places take my addiction to another level. You can sit in there and watch fifty to ninety races a day from around the country. When I signed my first NBA contract and was making around $700,000 a year, I'd play $20 across the board: win, place, and show. When I signed my second contract, that went up to $200 across the board, so $600 a race. Now I am playing $1,000 for just one race. If I have a bad streak, I go get more money. If I lose really bad, I walk out of there hating myself. Next day, I am right back at it. Gambling is one big mindfuck.

I have no interest in betting on sports of any kind. I think gambling on team sports is stupid. I never get into craps, either. But I do add another layer to my habit: blackjack. I'm up for anything that has the potential to appeal to my addictive personality, limited attention span, competitive edge, and total financial illiteracy. I play $1,000 a hand, three hands at a time, like it is nothing. If we are close enough to Atlantic City or Las Vegas, I get myself to a table. When we play in Chicago, I head out to Joliet, where they have a riverboat that can pull far enough off the shore that gambling is legal. They have similar setups in Florida. I have some great days in casinos, but I have more than my share of bad ones, too. That's how it is with degenerate gamblers. If you're a gambler, you're not a winner. Let's don't get it twisted.

Our son, Zeke, is born on October 20, 1992. Bridget is a hands-on mom from the start. I love every part of being a dad. Zeke is a real easy baby. When he is ten months old, he walks for the first time. When he starts talking, he has this perfect diction that you would never expect from a toddler. He says words like "actually" and it cracks me up.

Our team in Washington isn't real good, but we are young, and I love the guys. I also really like our coach, Wes Unseld. He is a Louisville guy, and he knows my dad some. As a player, Wes was known for his rebounding. He wasn't a vertical athlete, but he had a thick, strong body, and he knew how to use it. He was also known for his pinpoint outlet passes and a stoic demeanor. He is the same as a coach. He carries himself with class and strength, and though he doesn't say a whole lot, when he does speak, you know you better listen. He isn't much of a tactician. He coaches mostly by feel. More than anything, he expects you to play hard.

Wes is also hilarious and extremely likable. If we are flying to a game, all the players collect little bottles of Courvoisier cognac. Then we put 'em in a vomit bag, hand it to Wes and say, "Hey, let's don't practice tomorrow." It usually works.

I love sitting next to Wes on flights and buses. When he tells one of his stories from his playing days, I am riveted.

Wes is also a great shit talker. We end practices with some free-throw shooting. He walks around the court and chirps at us as we shoot. One day he comes up to me and says, "You're going bald just like your dad." The other guys crack up.

I think he is fucking with me, but after practice, I look closely in the mirror. Damned if he isn't right.

I have always worn my hair short. Over the next year, it gets thinner and thinner. I just shave it all off. My philosophy is, you have to make it look like you *want* to be bald. Too often, when guys lose their hair, they try to cover it up for too long. I can grow the bottom part out real long, but I can't grow anything on top.

I am the first of my friends to lose my hair, but it doesn't bother me. A lot of men in my family lost their hair relatively young. My uncle E.L. was the first person I knew to wear a toupee, and I thought it was hilarious—but not as hilarious as the day I was visiting home from Kentucky and saw that my dad had started wearing one as well. When he walked outside, I keeled over in laughter. I could not stop. Every time I composed myself, I'd start laughing again. I couldn't breathe. "All right, Rex, that's enough," my mom finally said. He wore that dumb thing for a couple of years while he was coaching. However I am gonna handle losing my hair, wearing a goddamn toupee is not going to be an option.

The thing about Wes, though, is he is a lot of fun, but

you can only push him so far. That man knows how to stand his ground. I see that one day in January when Bernard King comes into practice determined to be a major disruption. Bernard is coming off an injury and hasn't been cleared yet. He is trying to force the team to waive him. The Bullets are holding firm, so Bernard shows up to practice unannounced. Wes tells him he can't play, but Bernard comes onto the court anyway. "I'm fucking Bernard King!" he says.

Bernard jumps into practice and is intentionally messing up in the drills. He throws a ball into the stands. Finally, Wes has enough. He lunges at Bernard, grabs his jersey, and twists it around his neck. A few players and I jump in to break it up.

Wes comes into the locker room after practice. Bernard is sitting in there with us. "Bernard, you have to see the doctor before you can come back," Wes says calmly. "You're not even supposed to be in the locker room." Bernard talks some shit, but by then he is smart enough not to try to get physical with Wes. At any rate, Bernard accomplishes his mission. The Bullets waive him the next day, and he signs with the Nets.

● ○ ●

I go back to Lexington for the off-season and continue to work real hard, especially on getting my legs back and my body right. For the first time, I pay attention to my diet. I start my day early in the morning at UK with Kenny, Sam Bowie, and some other former Wildcats. We take pride in going at it hard with those young UK players. We bully them and show them what it takes to be pros. I know those guys are appreciative. Whatever has gone on with me and UK, I love feeling like I'm helping out my school.

When our workouts are done, I go to the track, although I tell Bridget I am out playing golf. Sam owns racehorses, and he and I are track buddies. After we are done gambling, we play some more pickup ball at night. There is double motivation at work. Yes, I am dedicating myself to basketball, but I also know that the more time I spend in the gym, the less I have to spend at home.

The season gets under way, and I feel great. I play great, too, averaging 18.2 points per game, a career high. We are due to play the San Antonio Spurs at the Baltimore Civic Center on January 17. The morning of the game, I get a call from Abe Pollin, the owner of the Bullets. He tells me he is with Wes, and they have just found out that I have made the Eastern Conference All-Star team as a reserve. "You're our first All-Star since Bernard King," Abe says. I am elated. After all that hard work, I am finally going to be recognized as one of the best players in the NBA.

My All-Star caliber play fuels another intriguing possibility—a trade to the Chicago Bulls. Michael has abruptly retired and is playing minor-league baseball, and they have replaced him with Ron Harper. David Falk tells me that the Bullets are in talks with Jerry Krause to work out a trade. The pressure is on for me to keep playing well.

The game tips off. Late in the first half, I drive to the basket and come down on Dennis Rodman's foot. I roll my ankle and feel a sharp pain, which is nothing new for me. I hit the ground. J. R. Reid, my old teammate with the Hornets, is sitting on the Spurs' bench, and I hear him say, "Oh shit!" I start to get up, but David Robinson puts his hand on my chest and says, "Don't."

That's when I look at my foot. It is turned at a gruesome angle. The bottom of my shoe is pointed toward my face. I am bleeding through my sock.

It hurts something awful, but the main thing I feel is embarrassment. I am supposed to be a great player with all this potential, and yet I keep getting hurt. All I want is to get the fuck off that floor.

The Bullets' trainers help me into the locker room. They do a quick X-ray, which reveals that I haven't broken anything. The ankle is just badly dislocated. The team doctor tells me he wants to try to pop the ankle back into place. He warns me it will hurt, but that the longer we wait, the harder it will be to pop it back in. If it doesn't work, they will try it again.

I tell him to go ahead. That motherfucker isn't lying. It hurts real bad. The second time hurts worse because I know what's coming. Both attempts fail, so they decide to send me to a hospital.

Besides being twisted and disgusting, my foot is also covered in blood because the bone has broken through the skin. Bridget and Zeke are there that night, and they come back to see me. Bridget can't stand the sight of blood, so she doesn't stay long. They send me to the hospital alone in an ambulance. There is a bad blizzard that night, so it takes more than two hours to get me to the hospital. Every time the driver tries a new route, he finds that it is closed off. It is just me and him in that ambulance, and I am in a lot of pain. I am quite a sight when they finally wheel me into the emergency room, my foot twisted and bloody, still wearing my uniform.

When the doctor finally comes to see me, he says they are gonna untwist my foot. "You're gonna knock me out, right?" I ask.

"You won't be out," the doctor replies, "but you won't remember it."

Next thing I remember, I am waking up in my bed at home in front of the TV, still wearing my uniform. There is an Aircast around my foot. The doctor was right, I don't remember a thing, but Bridget tells me she could hear me screaming from the waiting room.

● ○ ●

Caley Michelle Chapman is born on August 19, 1994. Our little home team is growing, but not much changes. Bridget is still an all-star mom. I am a good dad when I am around, but I find plenty of reasons not to be.

I might feel differently about being at home if things were going better for me at my job. Not that I am terrible or anything. I have some real high-level stretches in Washington, but every time I get rolling, I have another injury. I have great legs for jumping and terrible feet for landing. I have really high arches, which predispose me to rolling my ankles. If I'm not taped properly and I come down on someone's foot, I am gonna get hurt. Usually, it doesn't hurt too much when I roll it, but the next morning on the plane, the ankle will swell up badly, and I'll have to miss some more games. That, in turn, throws off my conditioning and rhythm, which makes me susceptible to getting hurt. It is a brutal cycle.

I also attribute some of my injuries to lack of sleep. When I was a kid, my bedtime was seven or eight o'clock, but I wouldn't fall asleep until ten or eleven. My dad was a huge stickler for being on time, so that added to my stress about oversleeping. I wouldn't have to wake up until 6:00 a.m., but I would set the alarm for 4:00 a.m. so I could hit the snooze button a bunch of times. My brain just runs too hot.

The problem gets worse as I get older. The travel that comes with being an NBA player doesn't help, although the one place where I sleep best is on an airplane. As soon as I hear the roar of that engine, I am out like a light. But we fly commercial. If we have back-to-back road games, that means taking the first flight out the next morning. There are lots of times when I play on two or three hours of sleep. It takes a toll on my body, but even worse is the damage it does to my mental health.

Wes resigns after we go 24-58, and he is replaced by Jim Lynam for the 1994–95 season. We get off to a great start, winning four of our first five games. Then we get drilled by 20 at Orlando. One of our new players is Scott Skiles, an exceptional point guard who had been traded to the Bullets that summer after playing the previous five seasons in Orlando. I loved watching Scott play at Michigan State, and he becomes one of my closest friends. Playing with him is a blast because I know he will fight anyone at any time.

Scott still owns a house in Orlando. Before the game, he invites all of us back there for a party. It is the best party I have ever been to. Girls are everywhere. People are swimming in the pool, drinking, dancing, having a great time. Our GM, John Nash, is there, which is awkward because there has been a lot of chatter in the press that he is about to trade Tom Gugliotta. I look over at one point and see Googs talking with John and smoking a cigarette. They are acting all friendly, until a bunch of guys grab John and throw him into the pool. He is not amused.

Our teammate Gheorghe Muresan is there, too. All season long we'd been calling him the Aardvark, but he didn't know why. One day he asked, and we showed him a picture of an aardvark with a long nose that looked just like his uncircumcised dick. So Gheorghe comes out of the house buck naked and yells, "Make way for the Aardvark!" Apparently, he has had quite a few beers. He is holding a can, which looks like a thimble in his enormous hand.

Gheorghe runs up to the pool and dives headfirst into the water. Unfortunately, the spot where he dives is only four feet deep, and Gheorghe is seven foot seven. Instantly there is blood everywhere. Having Gheorghe Muresan die in the pool will definitely be a party ender, but fortunately he has just scraped himself up. Gheorghe is fine, and a few days later John trades Googs.

After playing sixty games in each of my first two years in Washington, I play in just forty-five that year. I am never out for very long, just a few games here and there, but that adds up. When you're banged up as often as I am, you'll do anything to get back on the court. Give me a pill, shoot me up, whatever. I have been doing it since high school. I know that when I am healthy, I am good enough to make an All-Star team, and I want that chance again more than anything in the world.

The team is in a six-game losing streak in February when we are playing the Miami Heat at home. During a defensive possession, I reach out to deflect a pass, and the ball shatters the tip of my right thumb. It makes a loud cracking sound. I play the rest of the game, but the thumb hurts like hell and is badly disfigured. If I try to pull up my pants, I get a horrible shooting pain up my arm. After the game, they give me an X-ray and tell me it is broken. I am supposed to be out for six weeks, but I come back in less than three, which is epically stupid. It's real hard to play basketball with a half-broken thumb on your shooting hand.

I expect to be with the Bullets for a while. We had agreed to a contract extension right before the season. I find out otherwise the night of the 1995 NBA Draft, when I get traded to the Miami Heat, which has just brought in the legendary Pat Riley to be their head coach.

This is going to be my third team in eight years. I am only twenty-seven years old, and I believe that I have plenty of high-level basketball left to play. Moving around so much makes it harder to build a stable home, but such is the life of an NBA player. Things were more simple when it was just me, but now I have Bridget, Zeke, and Caley to look after. We pack up, head south, and start a new chapter as a family.

chapter

11

I know how demanding Pat Riley's training camps are, so I work my ass off to get ready. I am doing great until I start to feel a nagging pain in my right heel. An MRI reveals I have crepitus, which is when you have air trapped in the tissue under the skin. The bigger problem is that I have a lot of scar tissue around my Achilles tendon, which needs to be cleared out. For all my injuries, this is the first time I have to go under the knife.

The tricky part is recovering from the incision, because there's not a lot of skin in that area. Twice a day, I go into a hyperbaric chamber and sit alongside cancer patients, trying to get my ankle to heal. One day Pat comes over to me and says, "Hey, Rex, I know you want to be out there. Everybody knows it. But you're gonna be out for six weeks anyway. You've got a wife and two young kids at home. Take this time to be with them and relax as much as you can." It is great advice, and I take it.

I do my best to stay in shape while I am out, so when I come back I am ready to compete. All those years when I was putting up numbers on bad teams, there was a part of me that wondered if I was really that good. That season in Miami confirms it. I play fifty-six games and average 14 points in 33.3 minutes. I shoot 37.1 percent from three, which will end up being one of the highest clips of my career. That's what happens when you play with a great center like Alonzo Mourning, who constantly draws double teams. That means lots more open shots for the guards.

In late February, we have a big game at home against the Chicago Bulls. That team only loses ten games this season, but ours is one of them. I score 39 points. When I get home, I wake up Zeke and ask if he wants to sit on the couch with me and watch TV. We do this once in a while; it is our special quiet time. He is wearing his Michael Jordan jersey because he is a huge Bulls fan.

As we're watching TV, something clicks in his head. He turns to me and asks, "Didn't you play the Bulls tonight?"

I say yes.

"Did you win?" he asks.

I say yes again.

He runs upstairs crying and dives back into bed.

Five weeks later, we play the Bulls at home. I walk onto the court for the opening tip. As soon as that ball goes up,

Michael cracks me in the sternum with a hard elbow. I think, *Oh, shit, it's gonna be one of those nights.* Michael has 32 points, and he and his teammates hound me, so I score only 12 points on one of seven three-point shooting. We lose by 18. It isn't much better two nights later, where Michael has 40 points to my 16, and the Bulls win, 100–92. That dude is a killer.

I've played for a lot of good coaches whom I respected a lot, but I've never wanted to please a coach as much as I want to please Pat Riley. He is just as intense and detail-oriented as I expected. One night we are on the road, and Pat and I end up on the same elevator in our hotel. He turns to me and says, "Rex, I know I don't say much to you, but that's only because there are other guys on the team who need it more. You're a pro, and you know what you're doing, so I don't have to worry about you as much."

Pat Riley thinks I'm a pro? Man, that felt great.

We finish the season with a 42-40 record. It is my first time in the playoffs. I have been in the NBA for eight years, but until this moment, I have never played in a truly meaningful game. Unfortunately, our first-round opponent is the Bulls, and they sweep us en route to winning their first of three straight titles. This is a different Bulls team than I have seen before. They beat us like we are a jayvee team. I'm not sure they even break a sweat. It never feels good when a season ends, but I feel like the Heat are a team on the rise, and I am excited to help make that happen.

In the off-season, however, things get messed up. I had

one year left on my contract when the Bullets traded me to Miami. All season long Pat had assured me the team was gonna take care of me, but then they get into a huge bidding war to sign Juwan Howard, who is on the Bullets and is a free agent. The Heat are also trying to re-sign Alonzo Mourning, so their salary cap space is limited. David Falk represents all three of us, so it is an awkward situation. The Heat's solution is to ask me to take a one-year deal at the league's minimum salary, which is around $250,000. I had made $2 million the year before, so I refuse to go along. David and Pat both try to talk me into signing the deal, but I hold firm. I know I am better than that, and I am pissed that Pat misled me all season. Even when Miami raises its one-year offer to $900,000, I turn them down. So they renounce their rights to me, and I become a free agent.

I go back to Kentucky to go through my usual summer routine. Milwaukee has some money, but they just drafted Ray Allen, so they try to lowball me. I turn them down, thinking, *Fuck Ray Allen. Let's see how that turns out for them.* (It turns out well.) I am being hardheaded, which, given my injury history, I have no right to be. I figure, *Hey, I've got plenty of dough. I can just retire and spend the rest of my life playing golf and going to the track. What could go wrong?*

Toward the end of the summer, I get a call from Danny Ainge, who has just retired as a player and is now an assistant coach for the Phoenix Suns. I have always admired his competitiveness. He tells me he thinks they will have a good team with Kevin Johnson running the point, but they need a veteran shooting guard. The problem is they have very little cap space and need me to play for pretty close to the league minimum. He promises me that if things go well for me, which he thinks they will, then I will be rewarded. It is my last chance to play in the NBA that season, and I take it. The Chapmans are off to Phoenix.

● ○ ●

I am surprised at how reborn I feel in the desert. I have always heard about seasonal depression and the need for sunlight, but I never believed in it until I get here. The Suns have some really good young players like Mike Finley and Wesley Person, but they need a veteran to show them the way. I had tasted winning in Miami and want to taste some more.

One of the most intriguing players on our team is our rookie point guard, Steve Nash, who the Suns had drafted out of Santa Clara with the fifteenth pick. Our coach, Cotton Fitzsimmons, is skeptical at first. We are playing in an exhibition and Steve's man blows by him for a layup. Cotton turns to Danny, who is sitting behind the bench, and says in that gravelly voice, "Rook's awful slow, Aingie." We lose our first eight games, and Cotton quits. Danny takes over as coach, and we lose five more before getting our first win.

Playing for the Suns means living a lot closer to Las Vegas. If we have an off day, it is nothing for me to leave practice, meet a buddy at the airport, hop a quick flight, gamble, work out, and make it back that night. Sometimes I take Bridget and the kids with me. We stay in a huge penthouse with three bedrooms and have all the food we can eat. The kids go swimming during the day, and I'm in the casino all night. Everybody wins, except my bank account.

If I'm not going to Vegas, I am at the racetrack. I know that I will probably never make a dollar after I am through playing. Who would want to hire an ex-NBA player with no college degree? Yet I spend money like it will last forever. I have zero concept of financial responsibility. For example, we get licensing checks a couple of times a year. I'll come back to the locker room and there'll be a check made out to me for twenty-five grand. I cash it immediately and am off to the races—literally.

My financial advisor, Billy Wilcoxon, makes me feel like shit if I overspend for anything. He has warned me at least fifty times. "Son, let me tell you something," he drawls. "You're not gonna have a fucking penny. You're gonna be broke." Billy threatens to leave me a bunch of times, but he knows that I'll be the same way with someone else, so he tries to help as best he can.

I'm sure I am the worst client Bill has ever had. One time he tells me I have a million dollars in the bank. I think that is great until he reminds me, "You had to make *two* million to have that." *Oh yeah, right, taxes. Thanks, Bill!* It gets to where I even try to keep my money flow a secret from him sometimes. I figure out that if I go up to a bank and ask for a counter check, they will hand it to me straight out of my account. Then I can cash it and go to the track. Bill won't find out about it until the end of the month. I give him a warning a day or two in advance, and he makes me feel like I am stealing from him.

I keep all of this from Bridget. Sometimes she finds out what I've been doing and confronts me. It puts our marriage on an endless spin cycle. I give her a perfectly legitimate reason to complain about my behavior, and then I get pissed off that she is complaining. It all stems from the basic fact that I am unhappy with myself. I need some form of external excitement—basketball, gambling, golf, traveling, whatever— or I'll lose my mind. She can't give me any of these things. The only thing she can do is keep me from doing them. I grow to resent that.

There are plenty of times when I am happy at home. We do a lot together as a family. As long as the kids are around, Bridget and I can enjoy each other's company. Without them, it's harder.

Steve Nash and I become great friends. He is super smart and knows a lot about stuff other than basketball, like politics and business. Sometimes that can make for an awkward fit in an NBA locker room, but that is never the case with Steve because he is so likable. I love sitting next to him on the plane and picking his brain about what is going on in the world.

Steve isn't a traditional NBA athlete, but he is a terrific ball handler and his brain is special. He is also a terrific shooter. His misses are either long or short, rarely right or left. He is pudgy as a rookie, and I think he has the potential to be a solid NBA point guard. But I didn't predict he would be a future MVP, or even an All-Star. Anyone who says they did is lying.

Things really pick up the day after Christmas, when we make a big trade with the Mavericks that lands us Jason Kidd. I am shocked the Mavs gave him up because he had just become an All-Star. It is like playing with a six-foot-four Muggsy Bogues. I am in heaven. All I have to do is run as hard as I can downcourt and I know Jason will deliver me the ball where I can score. Instantly, we become a different team.

Personality-wise, Jason fits in great with me and Steve. We all live close to one another, drive to practices together, and play a ton of golf. However, there is tension between Jason and Kevin Johnson, which is weird because they both went to Cal. KJ is more political in his interactions—he eventually will become the mayor of Sacramento—but Jason is more blunt. One time during training camp, Steve is guarding KJ full-court, and KJ gets really pissed, and pretty soon we have to separate them. There is a period after that where Kevin doesn't want to practice with us at all. He goes off and shoots somewhere else instead.

I am rolling pretty good that first year in Phoenix, until I bust my right index finger in practice in late January. It gets caught in KJ's jersey and is badly dislocated. I try to pop it back in, which is a dumb move because I tear ligaments. I have surgery on the finger and miss three weeks. It sucks to be out of action, but it is good for my legs to get the rest.

We end up 40-42 and make the playoffs as the seventh seed in the West. That puts us against the No. 2 seed, Seattle. I love going up against the Sonics. They have Gary Payton and Hersey Hawkins in the backcourt. Both of them are great defenders, but I know they will be occupied with Jason and KJ and leave me with Detlef Schrempf. There is no way Detlef can guard me, although to be fair, I have a very hard time guarding him, too.

When I walk on the floor for game one, I am healthy, focused, confident, and ready to go. I get in the zone and never come out of it. By the time the game is over, I have made 9 three-pointers, an NBA playoff record, and end up with 42 points in a 106–101 win.

We split the next two games, giving us a 2-1 advantage heading into game four at home. The game is competitive from the start. When we trail by 3 points with 4.3 seconds to play, it looks like the Sonics are about to even things up. Danny calls time-out and draws up a play in the huddle. The first option is KJ. I am the second. As Danny is going over the play, Jason and I make eye contact. He gives me a look and a nod that says, *Be ready. I'm coming to you.*

Jason inbounds the ball from the sideline just in front of half-court. I am in the middle of the floor. I sprint away from the ball. Jason throws a high pass. My first thought is that it is gonna sail out of bounds. I sprint toward the opposite sideline and manage to catch it. It is like the ball has fallen out of heaven and right into my hands.

Problem is, I am running away from the rim when I catch

it. I am worried that Hersey is gonna foul me, which would take away the three. He puts his hand on my hip and gives me a little shove, but not hard enough to be called. I turn, jump, and shoot as quickly as I can. In that instant, I think, *If this doesn't go in, it's a terrible shot.*

Swish. Overtime. My teammates swarm me. The fans go nuts.

A lot of people clamp up in situations like this, but for me, this has always been my comfort zone. I think a big part of that is my ADD mindset. With my mechanics and touch, I should be a 90 percent free-throw shooter. Yet, my career percentage is 80, because I can't concentrate hard enough most of the time. But put me on the line late in the game in a high-pressure situation, and I am totally locked in. I've played on teams with guys who were better free-throw shooters, but if we got a technical foul, the coaches almost always gave me the free throws.

The same is true for late-game possessions. Often, I'll be bored the first three quarters, like I am waiting to see how the movie is going to end. Then, when the last few minutes arrive, I get hyperfocused. It doesn't matter if I am 0 for 10 up to that point. I want that ball.

It helps your confidence when you've had success in those moments. I've been making shots like that since grade school. I did it in a high school game I played at Memorial Coliseum when I was a senior. There were close to ten thousand people there. I scored about 40 points, including a game-winning eighteen-footer at the buzzer. It was the most natural thing in the world, making that shot.

When I was at Kentucky, everybody was gunning for me, and I made big shot after big shot. I played for Team USA with a pair of future number one picks in Danny Manning and David Robinson. Yet, when we got into late-game situations and really needed a bucket, they came to me several times. I know how to square up against a defender, elevate, pump fake, shoot a runner—whatever the moment requires, I know how to score.

When I was real young, my dad used to say to me, "You gotta be willing to be the goat to be the hero." In other words, you've gotta be willing to miss in a few of those situations if you want to experience the elation of making one. Not everyone wants that responsibility. I always do.

It is like my entire life has brought me to this moment against the Sonics. The best part about making the shot is the joy it brings to my teammates. Danny Manning runs out to hug me. Steve is a rookie and has barely played in the game, but he is going crazy as well. KJ and Jason jump all over me. It is as pure and wonderful a moment as I have ever had and will ever have on a basketball court.

Unfortunately, the shot only sends the game into overtime, and the Sonics end up beating us, 122–115. They beat us again the next game by 24 points to end the series.

● ○ ●

During a pickup game with the UK guys during the summer of 1997, I try to dunk the ball, but Nazr Mohammed, a freshman recruit, accidentally undercuts me, and I fall on my right wrist. I don't want to get it X-rayed, but it hurts so bad I have to get it checked out. It is fractured. A Lexington doctor performs the surgery and puts in a screw. I don't even tell the Suns about it until I get to training camp. They are not happy.

That aside, and despite having turned thirty that October, I feel as good as I have felt in a long time. I am paid all of $326,700 in salary during the 1997–98 season, but I know my payoff is coming later. I earn every one of those league-minimum dollars. I play sixty-eight games and start sixty-seven, and I lead us in scoring at 15.9 points per game. We go 56-26—after losing our first thirteen—and get the No. 4 seed in the Western Conference.

In the game, however, we are playing Utah, and I pull my hamstring late in the second half. It feels like my leg is dead. We face San Antonio in the first round of the playoffs. I do everything I can to get right for the playoffs, but I have to miss the first game. I am dying to get out there. I get therapy all the time and sit in a hyperbaric chamber. I play in game two and am doing pretty well, but I tweak it again toward the end of the game.

For game three, I ask our team doctor to numb me up so I can give it a go. He gives me seventeen shots of Novocain and wraps me up tight. I manage to play, but the leg feels dead, and I have to come out. We lose, and two days later I watch from the bench as we get eliminated in game four. As the teams shake hands afterward, Gregg Popovich, the Spurs' coach, says to me, "I know this would have been a different series if you had played." It is nice of him to say, but I'm not sure if it makes me feel better or worse.

There is no reason to believe I can't keep up my momentum for several more years. However, I make a huge mistake before the start of the 1998–99 season when I switch shoe companies. I had worn Converse for my first five years in the NBA, and I did some subsequent deals with Nike. Those paid around $100,000 per year, which was good money. But a new company called AND1 wants to pay me big bucks to be one of the first players in the league to wear their stuff.

The start of the season is delayed because of an owners' lockout. Once the league and the union sign a collective bargaining agreement, the season gets under way in early February. Right away, I start having foot problems. One game, I am warming up and I think that one of my kids has put a coin in my shoe. I take the shoe off and fish around but find nothing.

It gets to the point where I have to take Novocain shots before most every game. Without those shots, there is no way I can play. It isn't the first time I've used a needle to get on the court.

Eventually I develop a condition in my right foot called Morton's neuroma. That's when the bundle of nerves at the end of your foot gets inflamed. It feels like I have a big, sharp marble between my toes.

I can use the shots to get through the games, but I can't do it every day for practice. The doctor I visit says he can perform surgery, but that will mean missing a month of action. We decide to wait until after the season. In the meantime, I need to find another way to lessen the pain. So he prescribes me Vicodin. That is the trade name for hydrocodone, an opioid that can be effective against pain but is also highly addictive.

I have taken pills before, so I don't think much of it. I am a very old thirty-one-year-old man. I know I don't have many years left to play. I have just signed a new contract, and the Suns are paying me a lot of money. With all the shit I have done to get myself onto the court to that point, taking a few pills doesn't seem like any big deal. So that's what I do.

chapter

12

Between the pain in my foot and various other injuries, the 1998–99 season goes downhill quickly. I start every game, and there are times when I look like my old self—25 points against the Hornets, 22 against the Rockets, 23 against the Jazz—but those nights are getting fewer and further between.

On January 29, 1999, our daughter Tatum is born. Since it happens during the season, the parenting responsibilities fall mostly on Bridget, but that is nothing new. I finish out the season as best I can, but when the playoffs come, we get swept in three games by the Portland Trail Blazers. I score a total of 17 points in those games. I go through my usual off-season hoops-and-horse-racing regimen in Lexington, but I am in rough shape compared to my younger days.

For the Suns, the big move in the off-season is a trade

that brings us Penny Hardaway, who had made the All-Star game four times during his first five seasons with the Orlando Magic. During a preseason game against the Lakers, I find myself guarding a young Kobe Bryant in the post. He makes a baseline fake, I go for it, and before I know it, he is dunking on the other side of the rim. That kind of thing is happening more often. There are times during a game when I blow by my man and think I have an open path to the rim—and then just before I score, someone catches up to me and strips it away. That stuff never happened before.

I begin the season coming off the bench, move into the starting lineup in early December when Penny gets hurt, but I lose my spot in late January when Penny is healthy again. My ankle is in bad shape all season. I'll do routine slides during warm-ups and it rolls right over. I'll play the game and think it is fine, but then we'll fly somewhere, and by the time we land, it is all blown up.

My hand is really messed up, too. Over the previous few years, I have broken my thumb, index finger, and wrist. I can't spread my fingers real wide, which makes it difficult to control the ball. I am spending more time in the training room than on the practice court.

In mid-March, we are playing in Vancouver. I don't feel well all day and log just seven minutes. We fly to Oakland, where we are going to play the Warriors the next day. Caley is five years old, and she is traveling with me. When we get to my hotel room, I start to feel this really sharp pain in my abdomen. I think it is just some really bad gas, so I crawl into bed hoping it will go away. But it only gets worse. Finally, I call our trainer and say, "I think I need to go to the hospital."

Frank Johnson, who is an assistant coach, and his wife take care of Caley while I go to a local emergency room, where they diagnose me with appendicitis. They are worried my appendix is going to rupture, so they want to cut it out right away. The next night after the game, I fly with the team back to Phoenix. When I get off the plane, a doctor hands me a bottle of pills. "This will help with the pain," he says.

I look at the bottle. *OxyContin.* I have never heard of it, but the doc says I should take 'em. So I do.

Within two days, I am in love.

An appendectomy is just about the most basic, entry-level surgery you can have. I shouldn't have been given OxyContin for that. It doesn't hurt that bad, but I keep taking the pills anyway because of how they make me feel. OxyContin gives me the same kind of high Vicodin did, only it is way more enjoyable. Every single thought that comes through my head is super positive, super optimistic. That is exactly the opposite of how I am used to thinking. I don't feel like I can fly or anything like that. It is just an overriding but firmly held belief that whatever problems come my way will eventually just go away.

It never occurs to me that I am becoming addicted. I mean, a doctor gave them to me, right? My judgment goes south quick. OxyContin and Vicodin are both opioids, but to me there isn't any comparison. OxyContin is just different, man. It's also time-released, so the high lasts a long time. The synthetic morphine hits you at different times throughout the day. That tricks my mind into believing that the stuff is actually safer than Vicodin. *Hey, I'm only gonna take just one, that's no big deal.*

It should be hard for me to keep getting so many pills, but it isn't. We will be in some NBA city, and I can call a doctor and say, "I'm Rex Chapman, I play for the Phoenix Suns. Can you write me a prescription?" Most every time, they say sure. There is no coordinated reporting system, so I can hop from doctor to doctor and get what I need. I even go to my dentist from time to time to restock.

It's summertime and I am barely around the team, so there is no way any of my teammates or coaches on the Suns realize I am falling into an opioid addiction. I don't even realize it. I am resigned to the fact that my season is over, and I will just have to wait until next fall to get back on the court. It ends up being the only season in my career when I average under 10 points per game, and the first one since before high school in which I don't have a single dunk.

I am physically beat-up, but I think if I have another good off-season, I'll be ready to go. The pills say otherwise. You build up a tolerance real fast, so I have to increase my intake. Within a few months, I am taking six or seven OxyContins a day. Plus, it is getting harder to feel the Vicodin, so I think I have to ratchet that up as well.

There are short windows over the summer of 2000 where I think I can keep playing. The Suns are running all these tests on my hand. I'll go in the gym and shoot for a while and feel the muscle memory coming back, but I am half-assing it. Our trainer, Aaron Nelson, walks up to me one day, looks at my pot belly and glassy eyes, and cracks, "You look fucked up, man. In a few years, you're gonna be drooling." He says it as a joke, but he is at least half-serious, not to mention correct. The only thing I give a shit about is those opioids. It is the first time in my life that I want something more than basketball.

Late that summer, I get a call from Bryan Colangelo, the GM of the Suns. He asks if I plan on coming to training camp. "I don't think so," I say. Just like that, my playing days are done.

I've spent twelve years in the NBA, and by many measures, I've had a very successful career. But I know it wasn't all it could have been, had I been healthier and made better decisions along the way. When it finally ends, it could have been a jarring, emotional, upsetting moment, but I don't feel any of these things. I'm not feeling much of anything. The only thing I know for sure is that I am gonna keep taking the medicine, and that sounds all right to me.

● ○ ●

Retirement is a massive life change. I'm not prepared for it in the slightest. I have given exactly zero thought to my post-playing future. I have no plans, no dreams, no goals, no idea of what I will do with the rest of my life. Through my opioid fog, I figure I'll just go to the track and play golf and see my kids do all the stuff I missed while I was playing.

Since I technically retired due to injuries, the Suns have to pay me the balance of my contract. That means $13 million is coming my way during the four years after I am done playing. Combine that with the $5 million or so I have in cash and other assets, and I am sure I have plenty to last me the rest of my life.

I blow through that money so fucking fast. I was never good with money in the first place, but now it is a hundred times worse because I am on OxyContin. I don't have practices or games to go to, so it is easy for me to spend all my time at the track or head off to Vegas for days at a time. I go to a bank in Phoenix and get a million-dollar loan just so Bridget and my financial folks can't keep track of my spending. Another time I show up to a casino short of cash, so they offer to give me a marker. That means looping in Bill Wilcoxon. He is adamantly against me getting markers, but as always I remind him, it is my money, and if he doesn't help me get those markers, I will find someone who will. Bill tells me all kinds of stories about athletes who blew their cash and were left with nothing, but I just shrug him off and say, "That's not gonna be me."

Never underestimate the ability of an addict to rationalize destructive behavior. When I was in the NBA, I'd go several months without gambling a dime. *See that? I don't have a problem. I can stop any time.* But those periods never lasted long. Now that I'm not playing, it's even worse. I also think, stupidly, that I can hide my habit from my family. One day, when Zeke is eight or nine years old, he is riding with me in the car as I pull into a service station. While I am gone, he finds a bunch of my racing tickets. Zeke is just starting to get into math at school, so he is fascinated by all the numbers.

He adds everything up and figures out that I had lost about thirty grand in a single day. He is so proud of himself when I get back in the car and he can show what he has done. I feel like the worst fucking dad who ever lived.

One time I get a $400,000 cashier's check for a trip to Vegas. I hop a plane from Phoenix, take a cab to the Bellagio, cash the check, gather my chips, and take a seat at the black-jack table.

Forty-five minutes later, I am down to four grand. It gets so bad that even the dealers are feeling sorry for me. I am playing three hands at a time, but I only have money for one. What else can I do? I put my last four large on the table.

Blackjack.

An hour later, I have run my stake back up to $396,000. I am smart enough to take my money and leave, but pretty soon I am right back at it. That's OxyContin. It makes you feel invincible. It's the biggest lie there is.

Our daughter Tyson is born on October 29, 2000. As with all our kids, this is an unplanned pregnancy. I am in the de-livery room, but it is rough because Bridget and I are in such a bad place. I am in a permanent opioid haze, and things are getting darker by the day. It is almost like the Vicodin is an appetizer, and the OxyContin is the main course. The buzz is so good, I just chase it and chase it.

By the end of the year, I am up to nine or ten OxyCon-tins a day and forty Vicodins. I hide pill bottles everywhere, including under my mattress for when I wake up in the mid-dle of the night with bad cravings. When that happens, I roll over, grab a couple of Vicodins, chew 'em up, and go right back to sleep.

I know I have an issue, but I don't consider myself an addict. This is medicine, not drugs. I figure it isn't anything I can't handle. I am extremely lucky I do not drink alcohol, so I haven't added that to the mix.

As if all this isn't enough, I'm allergic to codeine, which is in Vicodin. If I have a certain amount, I start to itch. Once that itch comes, I know I have had enough. The codeine doesn't make me sleepy, but it's not a pick-me-up, either. None of this medicine does that for me. If it did, I wouldn't like it so much. My brain always runs too hot. But it all makes me feel real, real good, for the most part, and it helps me redirect my thoughts away from the stuff I hate to think about.

With basketball done and my addiction to opioids in full bloom, my judgment has gone all to hell, and I am unfaithful to my wife. Being unfaithful requires being mentally sharp so you can cover your tracks and remember your lies. That isn't the case with me. I am using a second flip phone, except it is the same kind as my first phone, and I often forget which is which. In early 2001, Bridget hires a private investigator and confronts me with the evidence he has collected. Instead of admitting what I have done, I get angry at her for tailing me. I use that as an excuse to spend even more time away from the house, as if my cheating is all her fault.

Bridget should leave me. It probably would be best for me, too. But we were both brought up in a conservative southern environment where it is a real stain to get divorced. When I was a kid I'd hear about married couples splitting up, and I'd think it was just about the worst thing I could imagine. So we keep trying.

● ○ ●

The main challenge when you're a drug addict is finding ways to get more drugs. It is an ever-present source of stress because you know the last thing you can do is stop taking those pills. I jump from doctor to doctor, and from pharmacy to pharmacy, but I need a better strategy.

When you decide you need to find a drug dealer, a drug dealer is easy to find. A mutual friend sets up a meeting for me with a guy in Tucson. I drive down in my Porsche 911 Turbo and meet the dealer in a parking lot behind a Walgreens in a strip mall. He looks like a bodybuilder on steroids. We are there for about fifteen minutes when a guy comes out of the Walgreens wearing a white pharmacy coat. He hands us two 500-quantity bottles of OxyContin. That keeps me in stock for a while. When I need more, now I know where to get it.

I drive back to Phoenix doing 110 miles an hour. This is epically stupid, because if a cop discovers what I have, I'll go straight to prison. No one would believe any single person could take all these pills, so I could be looking at felony charges for intent to distribute.

One of the side effects from the medicine is that it makes me sweat like crazy. I have these insane hot flashes during the day. I try to clean myself up with a handkerchief, but I'll still be drenched. Plus, I am gaining weight real fast, so my clothes are extra tight.

Opioids are not like alcohol, where you're stumbling drunk. You can drive and work and do all sorts of normal activities. That's why they have such big pill problems in coal mines and factory jobs: you can still perform. The rationality is part of the sickness. You convince yourself you're not drunk, but you are intoxicated on those pills. And you can't fucking live without them.

I think I am doing a good job hiding all this from my close friends and family, but it is obvious to them that I am on a bad path. Danny Ainge, who quit as the Suns coach twenty games into my final season, is the one who finally confronts me. He and I play golf a couple times a week, and our wives are good friends. Danny calls me in January 2001 and asks if I can come see him. I go over to Danny's house, and we sit together on his couch. I weigh 220 pounds, which is a good 30 pounds above my last playing weight, and I haven't been retired a year.

Danny gives it to me straight. "Look at you," he says. "You're a mess." He goes through all the areas of my life that I am mismanaging, one fucking disaster after another.

I don't even try to argue. The words hit me real hard coming from him. I've always thought of Danny as this happy, almost silly kind of guy, but he has always seemed very mature to me. We're different in a lot of ways—he never cusses, for one. I know if he feels this way, then he must be right. And I am ready to do something about it.

With Bridget's help, I find a rehabilitation center in Arizona called Sierra Tucson. I drive down there in February in my blue turbo Porsche going about 120 on the highway. There's no reason to speed my way to rehab. I'm just always in a fucking hurry. I know this is going to be my last chance to take any pills, so I chew a bunch on the way. I am about a mile from the facility when a scary feeling comes over me. It feels like my brain is short-circuiting. I pull over into a shallow ditch and black out. I'm not sure how long I am there. Could be five minutes, could be an hour. It's a miracle I don't die.

I somehow make it to Sierra Tucson and check in. It takes a while for me to fill out the forms and do all the administrative stuff. During a shift change, I can hear one nurse explain to her replacement that I have been admitted for addiction to OxyContin. "It's just like when they're coming off heroin," she says.

Heroin?

I cannot believe what I am hearing. Sure, I have gotten hooked on pills, but I'm not a fucking heroin addict.

Or am I?

They move me into detox. I have no idea just how bad that will be. By the second day, I am vomiting and sweating nonstop, thrashing around, trying to sleep, trying to keep my mind clear. One second you're hot as fuck, another you're cold as fuck. It is pure hell. The nurses give me some medicine to take the edge off, but I am as sick as can be.

It is a good ten days before that hell is over. Once it is, though, I feel as clear-minded as I have been in a long time.

When I replay everything I have done, the shame is overpowering.

I stay for thirty days. My room has no TV, the cafeteria has shitty coffee, and we are required to turn the lights out at 8:00 p.m. I attend group therapy meetings. It is eye-opening to hear some of the stories from the other patients. It is also terrifying. A few of the patients have gauze on their wrists and marks around their necks from suicide attempts. People are in there for all kinds of reasons, including anorexia and bulimia. These folks wear special wristbands so the staff will know they need to eat a certain amount. It's heartbreaking.

One day I am in a session, and as usual, the newcomers start out by explaining to the group why they have checked in. A woman stands up and confesses that she is a sex addict. She points right at me and adds, "And I want to fuck the shit out of him right now." It is kind of funny, I suppose, and no, I don't take her up on it. I share a lot in these group sessions, and during my daily individual therapy sessions as well. It feels good to have somebody to talk to.

During my stay at Sierra Tucson, I am diagnosed with attention deficit disorder and depression. I suppose I have been clinically depressed all my life, but it has gotten real bad since I stopped playing. The doctors prescribe me antidepressants. They help.

All in all, rehab is a really good experience, but super humbling. It is just what I need to get a fresh start. Some people get real anxious when they get close to their date of departure, but when my time is up, I look forward to trying to make things right with my family.

Most of all, I am happy to be off drugs.

● ○ ●

When I retired from the Suns, Jerry Colangelo told me that if I ever wanted a job, they'd have a place for me in the organization. As usual, he is true to his word and hires me as a college scout. I am also invited to audition with Turner Sports for a chance to do some color commentary on games. The audition goes well, and they hire me. I work games with Dick Stockton, John Thompson, and some others, and really enjoy it. I also make sure everyone with the Suns and Turner knows I have been in rehab. They are kind enough to grant me their trust, and I intend to keep it.

Now that I am off the medicine, I decide I really want to get right physically. For a time, I am thinking, *Hey, I'm only thirty-three, thirty-four years old, maybe I can get myself back into playing shape.* I start working out harder with that goal in mind.

One of the many things holding me back is a lingering pain in my right wrist. I still have a screw in there from when I had broken it a couple years before. I talk to the doctors about it, and they say it will be no problem to take the screw out.

When I go in for the surgery, I am asked if I am allergic to any medication. I answer honestly and say no. I do not mention that I am an addict and that I should not be given any pain meds. They perform the surgery and write me a prescription for Vicodin. I get it filled and wait a few days, thinking maybe I won't take the pills after all. But my wrist is hurting pretty bad, so I figure, *What the heck, I'll only take one.*

It is goddamn amazing.

chapter

13

I t only takes a few days for me to get addicted to Vicodin again. It isn't hard to keep my supply up. If I run up against a doctor who doesn't want to overprescribe me, all I have to do is ask a different doctor to send the prescription to a different pharmacy. When you get addicted, you become a really good liar. Besides, people tend to give well-known former athletes what they want.

By early 2002, I am a mess again. I finally tell Bridget that I am back on the Vicodin. She doesn't give me any shit. She just starts working the phones. I am adamant that I don't want to go back to a traditional rehab place. I know I need to get off the meds, but that 12-step stuff is not for me. Too much God talk.

We find a place in Newport Beach, California, that specializes in detox. The place is like a country club. People can pretty much leave when they want. There is no therapy, no meetings, no doing the real work required to get control of your addiction. They hook me up to IVs for a few days to flush out my system. After a week or so, I am back in Phoenix.

This time, I am determined to stay off medicine for good. As soon as I get home, however, I develop an ache right below my sternum. It isn't a sharp pain, but it is constant, and very uncomfortable. The only thing that gives me relief is to clutch a pillow. At first, I think it is all in my head, but it seems pretty clear that I am going through withdrawal.

I see a couple of different doctors to find out what is happening. One of them recommends I start taking Suboxone. The drug, buprenorphine, was just approved by the FDA a couple of months before. It is designed to help people break their addiction to opioids and heroin. I take the medicine and—bam!—the pain goes away. It is so good to get some relief. I don't like having to take any kind of medicine, but I am willing to try anything for a chance at a somewhat normal life.

● ○ ●

After I get out of detox, I get promoted by the Suns to be their director of basketball operations. The team cycles through a couple of coaches after Danny, but we seem to have found something special in Mike D'Antoni. He loves to play run-and-gun basketball. We decide we need an upgrade at point guard to run Mike's attack.

Bryan Colangelo decides that there is only one candidate for us, and that is Steve Nash. The Suns had traded Steve on draft night in 1998 to the Dallas Mavericks in return for Martin Müürsepp, Bubba Wells, the draft rights to Pat Garrity, and a first-round draft pick. Steve had blossomed into a two-time All-Star in Dallas while playing for Don Nelson. Steve is becoming a free agent, and we've remained the best of friends. I assure Bryan and his right-hand man, Dave Griffin, that Steve's not just using us to get more money from the Mavericks. Bryan makes the deal. We also want to sign Quentin Richardson to give Steve another strong, athletic wing he can run with, but we don't have enough cap space to do it. The team goes to Steve and asks if he will take a million bucks off his salary so we can add Quentin. He says it is no problem.

Steve comes to Phoenix at exactly the right time. We have a core of exciting, young, athletic wings in Shawn Marion, Joe Johnson, and Amar'e Stoudemire, who fit perfectly in Mike's system. Not only do we make the Western Conference Finals in 2005 but Steve wins the first of his two MVP trophies. I am in the car with him when he gets the call from NBA commissioner David Stern. Steve immediately calls his brother, Marty, who is a really good basketball player in his own right and is now playing professional soccer. When Steve shares the news, Marty replies, "You're so fucking lucky I didn't play basketball."

I should be feeling lucky, too. But I'm not. Three years after I was first given Suboxone, I am still taking the medicine.

I don't think of Suboxone as a "real" opioid, or something you could get addicted to. I take it because if I don't, that pain in my abdomen will come back in full force. People are only supposed to be on Suboxone for a couple of months. I am long past that now, with no end in sight and no doctor to tell me otherwise.

The Suboxone takes its toll on me in subtle ways. I've never been one for managing details, but now I am genuinely dazed and confused. Like, my driver's license expired in 2004. It's real easy to renew a driver's license, but I never do. I get pulled over by the cops a few times for speeding or whatever. Sometimes they let me go, sometimes they give me a ticket, and a couple of times they impound my car. I go to court to get the license back, but eventually I get another letter saying it is suspended. I toss it in the trash.

I don't get suddenly whacked out of my mind when I am on Suboxone. It is more like a steady, creeping deterioration. I almost don't realize what is happening. My doctors assure me it isn't addictive, and I have convinced myself it's only for my arthritis. But if I go a day or two without taking it, I get really sick.

● ○ ●

During my work with the Suns, I travel to Stillwater, Oklahoma, to scout some players who play for Oklahoma State. The coach there is Eddie Sutton. Eddie and I did not part Kentucky on good terms, to say the least, but I've long said that if I didn't have those two years under Eddie to learn his defensive principles, I would not have lasted in the NBA. If Eddie had stayed on as coach at Kentucky, we probably would have spent some time together as adults and gotten past all that friction, but his firing removed whatever connection we had.

When I get on campus, I make a point to go see him. It is a really nice visit. We talk a little about what went on between us, and I feel like we patch things up. I am really glad for that.

I think the Suns are getting close to putting together a team that can win a title, but we let Joe Johnson walk and sell the eighth pick in the draft, which turns out to be Andre Iguodala. I argue vehemently against these moves. I am becoming increasingly impatient and irritable. When Kevin McHale asks if I want to be a personnel scout for the Minnesota Timberwolves, where he is the GM, I take the opportunity to make my exit. I have always liked Kevin, and working there will mean being reunited with my old Kentucky coach Dwane Casey, who is the team's head coach.

I get a hotel room in Minnesota and split my time between there and Phoenix. The Timberwolves have Kevin Garnett but not much else. We go 33-49 that season. I think I'll stay in Minnesota for a while, especially with Dwane there, but late in the 2005–06 season, I get a call from an old Kentucky buddy named Bret Bearup. Bret was a backup during his four years with the team in the early 1980s. He was never gonna play pro basketball, but he is a brilliant guy who went on to have great success in the financial industry. He has become real tight with Stan Kroenke, the owner of the Denver Nuggets, and is working full-time for the team. Bret calls to ask if I'll sign on as the Nuggets' VP.

Bret invites me to meet with him and Stan in the South of France. I am there for two weeks, and we have a lot of fun. It doesn't take much to convince me. I might have a foggy brain, but I know a good opportunity when I see it.

● ○ ●

Bret and I rent a condo overlooking Coors Field and live there together. The Nuggets have an interesting team, but we have a lot of work to do.

Carmelo Anthony is in his third year in the league, and he is blossoming into an elite scorer. Defensively, the pillar of the franchise is Kenyon Martin, whom the Nuggets had acquired in a trade with the Nets in 2004. Kenyon is one of my favorite people ever. He has one of the most dominant locker-room personalities I have ever been around. He laughs a lot, but you know never to fuck with him. The team found that out in one of his first practices, when Kenyon punched Nenê in the face. Nenê had to be restrained, which is crazy because Nenê is one of the sweetest guys you could ever meet. It is beautiful to watch the two of them play together.

Kenyon played with Jason Kidd in New Jersey, so we bond immediately. He stuttered badly as a kid, and he got teased for that. I ask him when the teasing stopped. He waits what seems like a long time and finally answers, "When I started beating their ass."

We also have a super coach in George Karl. I ask Bret what George is like. "George needs a lot of 'attaboys,'" he replies. I am surprised to hear that, but then I think, *Who doesn't need some attaboys from time to time?* George has a unique way of relating to players, and he likes to have a loyal crew around him.

George is real tight with Mark Warkentien, who was recently promoted to vice president of basketball operations. It isn't long before Mark and I are at odds from time to time. Both of us have strong opinions and strong personalities, and I have the added complication that my brain is becoming increasingly cloudy because of the Suboxone.

The only reason we make it work, sort of, is because Bret is good friends with both of us. Mark, to me, is a talent guy above all else when it comes to evaluating players. I agree with him on the importance of ability, but I also look harder for intangibles. We have a lot of tough guys on our roster, including reserves like Reggie Evans and Eduardo Nájera. In my view, anyone we bring in needs to fit into that mix.

Despite the differences between Mark and me, we and Bret bring in some really good players. That includes the blockbuster trade we make in December that lands us Allen Iverson from the Sixers. We have to give up Andre Miller and Joe Smith in that deal. Andre is a really good point guard, but he barely talks. I approach Andre at practice, sit him down, and say gingerly, "We just traded you to Philly for Allen Iverson."

Andre shrugs his shoulders, says, "Okay," and leaves.

Allen is in his tenth season in the NBA, and he is still putting up some crazy numbers. He can party all night and still get 40 the next day. He averages nearly 25 points per game, but we finish 45-37 and lose in the first round to the Spurs. Still, we have exceeded everyone's expectations. At the end of the season, Mark is named the NBA's executive of the year. I actually get one vote, which I'm pretty sure comes from Danny Ainge, who by then is running the Celtics.

● ○ ●

Very few people at the Nuggets know I am taking Suboxone. To me, it is just some medicine that has been given to me by a doctor. It remains a challenge to keep myself in stock, but as is always the case with addicts, where there's a will, there's a way. You can find doctors anywhere, especially if you're a former NBA player. The whole industry is a fucking pill mill.

Bridget knows I am taking Suboxone, but as usual, I keep the worst details to myself. I also keep up my gambling habit. On the days I am in Denver, I go to the local OTB early in the morning, place all my bets, drive to the office, and watch practice or do whatever it is I need to do, and then stop by the OTB on my way home to see how I did. If I'm not working, I can sit home all day on the couch and watch the races on DirecTV. Bret thinks I am nuts.

The flight from Denver to Phoenix is only about an hour, so it is easy to go back and forth to see Bridget and the kids. Still, there is no denying that during the season I am living in one place, and they are in another.

Bridget and I are in a really bad state. Shit, we have been in a bad state for several years, probably longer. We argue constantly. The kids are getting older, and they can tell things aren't right. Thank goodness for the kids. I love being involved in their lives—when I am around, anyway. I get the girls ready for their cheerleading competitions by wrapping their ponytails and helping them get dressed. Zeke is also starting to come into his own as a basketball player. I almost never miss one of his games. As he starts to move through the ranks, I talk to him about what is coming. "If you play, the crowds are gonna be on your ass about being my son," I say. "They're gonna taunt you and say a lot of mean things."

"I don't care," he replies.

Zeke might be mild-mannered when you talk to him, but when it comes time to compete, he is fearless. The road fans jeer him and chant, "Daddy's boy!" and he doesn't give a *fuck*. He likes it—and I like that he likes it. When those fans get on him, I see Zeke's face light up. I know the other team is in trouble.

If Zeke plays poorly, I let him know it. Most times he doesn't want to hear from me, but I say my piece anyway. Bridget steps in and says, "You know after a couple of minutes, he tunes you out." I know she is right because I was the same way with my dad. I don't want to repeat that dynamic with Zeke, so I back off, for the most part.

Zeke rebels like most teenagers do. Steve Nash is his idol, so he grows his hair like Steve's, with the headband and everything. I give Zeke a hard time about it, so he goes and gets it cut. I still think it is too long.

I bitch about this to Steve. "Zeker won't cut his fucking hair, and it's pissing me off," I say, using the nickname Steve has given him.

Steve rolls his eyes. "Rex, it's hair. Pick your battles, dude."

One of the great things about watching your kid play sports is sharing that pleasure with the family. Zeke will do well in a game, and I will call my dad or Bridget's dad, who are both ex-coaches, and they will be so jacked up about it. One time, I can't go to an AAU tournament that Zeke is playing in, so Bridget's dad takes him. He calls me and says, "You're not going to believe this. He's scoring on Harrison Barnes."

It is the same thing if one of the girls does well in a dance competition. As soon as we get in the car, we call Bridget's parents and tell them about it. Then we go out to dinner and relive what happened. I marvel at what wonderful young people Bridget and I are raising despite all the shit going on between us.

The only thing I've ever really wanted in life is to be a good dad. I am grateful that there are at least a few moments where I genuinely feel like one.

chapter

14

With my marriage as shitty as ever, and with my head becoming foggier by the day, I do my best to throw myself into my job with the Nuggets. Over the summer of 2008, we sign Chris "Birdman" Andersen to a free-agent contract. Chris had been suspended for a season for violating the NBA's substance abuse policy, and he basically hasn't played in two years. He is like a white Dennis Rodman. His skin is all tatted up, and what he lacks in skill he more than makes up for in tenacity and effort.

You never know what is gonna come out of Chris's mouth. One day I invite Junior Bridgeman to talk to our team. Junior was a star at Louisville, played twelve years in the NBA, and went on to make hundreds of millions of dollars, mostly by investing in fast-food restaurants.

"So what are your aspirations beyond basketball?" Junior asks.

Chris raises his ink-filled arm and answers, "My lifelong dream is to own a rest stop."

As the season gets underway, it is apparent that Allen is not quite the same player. He just doesn't have that burst. Most of us think he will get better, but Bret is the first to say he has changed for good. So we trade Allen to Detroit in return for Chauncey Billups. This is Chauncey's second go-round in Denver. He first came via a trade in 1999, but the Nuggets dealt him a year later to Orlando. Chauncey has bounced around through Minnesota and Detroit before returning to Denver. I am surprised the Pistons trade him, because he has played in multiple All-Star games and was the NBA Finals MVP in 2004.

Chauncey gives us a vocal, veteran presence, which our guys need. Carmelo is our leading scorer, J. R. Smith puts up 15 points a game, Nenê and Kenyon do their thing down low, and Birdman gives us amazing energy off the bench. We get past the Hornets and Mavericks in the first two rounds of the playoffs and end up facing the Lakers in the Western Conference Finals. Kobe Bryant is trying to win his first NBA title without Shaquille O'Neal, and when Kobe puts his mind to something, it is awfully hard to deny him. We lose in six.

The team brings back pretty much the same roster, and I think we have a chance to win a championship in 2010. We win fifty-four games, just one fewer than the year before, but we get upset by the Jazz in the first round of the playoffs.

A couple weeks after the season ends, I am home in Phoenix when I get a call from Paul Andrews, the team's CFO. "I'm sorry, Rex," he says, "but we're not renewing your contract."

Not renewing? I am floored. Up until that point, we had been talking about an extension. I am even more shocked to learn that they aren't retaining Mark, either. We knew that Stan Kroenke's son, Josh, who is one of my favorite people, was going to be taking a bigger role in the management of the franchise, but we both felt like we were a part of those plans. Turns out we were wrong.

I hang up. Bridget is standing there looking at me. She can tell before I say anything the news isn't good.

That kind of bad break would jolt any marriage, but for one already teetering on the edge, it is more than we can take. That fall, I take Zeke for his freshman year at Ball State, where he has been recruited for basketball. I help him unpack and go back to my hotel. The phone rings. It is Bridget.

"I want a divorce," she says.

She has said this many times before—we have both said it—but this time she adds, "I've hired a lawyer." That's how I know she is serious. I make a show of trying to talk her out of it, arguing we should keep trying for the sake of the kids, but her mind is made up. I guess part of me wants this, too, but it is still depressing. I have no job, no career, no prospects, and now I am about to have no wife. I feel like a total fucking failure.

● ○ ●

When I get back to Phoenix, I move into our guesthouse. A few days later, I check into a hotel. The divorce gets ugly real fast, as divorces tend to do. Not surprisingly, the central point of contention is money. It is clear from the get-go that Bridget's lawyer is going to aggressively protect her financial interests.

I am furious that they are doing this, but it is obviously the right thing to do on her part. Between my addiction to Suboxone, my gambling habit, and all the other stupid shit I spend money on, our dough is never gonna last if she doesn't grab all she can. We blow through hundreds of thousands of dollars in legal fees and build up a lot of anger toward each other sorting everything out. I am very, very bitter.

Finally, one of the divorce attorneys says to us, "Have you guys thought about trying mediation?" *What's mediation?* We try it, and the case is settled in a week. We could have saved so much time, money, and hurt feelings if we had gone to mediation at the start, but for some reason, the attorneys never thought to make the suggestion.

The divorce is finalized in 2013. After all those years, Bridget and I are finally, officially done.

● ○ ●

I rent myself an apartment in North Scottsdale. Zeke is away at college, and Bridget and I share fifty-fifty custody of the girls. Caley is a senior in high school, and she is driving. I tell her she can stay wherever she wants and doesn't need to worry about being at my place half the time, although she is always welcome and I love being with her. Tatum and Tyson are in middle school, so their visits are more regulated. The situation is hard to manage considering that Bridget and I are not speaking to each other.

When money gets tight, I sell a few cars. I try to convince myself I am still being a good dad. I love my kids very much, but I am not engaged like I should be. If I was in anything close to my right mind, I would tell them to just stay with their mom all the time. It isn't good for them to be around me.

I stop talking to my family and a lot of my friends. I check in with my parents here and there, but they are short conversations and not at all meaningful. Lots of times they call or text, and I don't answer.

I'm not actively looking to cut people off. I just stop answering or returning their calls. They'd only ask me how I am doing, and I'd have to lie and say I am okay.

Of course, I don't *have* to lie. I could tell them the truth. I could tell them I am not okay. But I am too ashamed, confused, and full of pride, still holding on to the last bits of my King Rex bullshit.

I keep taking Suboxone, rationalizing all the way. It is still a medically prescribed medicine. Helps me with my arthritis, too. It's not *really* an opioid. Besides, it isn't like I am gonna overdose. If I take too much of it, I get a huge headache. As far as I am concerned, everything is on the up and up.

Once a month, I go to the doctor. They are supposed to do blood and urine testing, but that hardly ever happens.

They check my blood pressure, maybe listen to my heart with a stethoscope or some bullshit, and write the prescription. Then I go to the pharmacy, pay my 150 bucks, and am all set for the month. I know I've made more than my share of mistakes, but these doctors fuck me. They are legal drug dealers.

Now and then, reality sets in, and the darkness covers me completely. *This is how it's always gonna be the rest of my life. I am never gonna be off this fucking medicine.*

One of my few remaining, quote-unquote, pleasures are my visits to the OTB down the street. It is the closest thing I have to a job. I spend hours at home handicapping the races. Sometimes I'll go over the racing forms while my girls are doing their homework. When morning comes, I take them to school, circle back to the OTB to place my bets, and then go home to watch the races on TV. I even make the girls wait in the car sometimes while I go inside. To them, me going into an OTB is like other dads buying gas. Normally, I play between $7,500 and $15,000. Some days I win thirty grand, and that lasts me a couple of weeks. Once in a while, I win real big, like a hundred grand. That is even worse. It's classic fool's gold.

Nobody in the NBA calls to express the slightest interest in hiring me. I might be able to find a job if I put myself out there and make some calls, but I am not in the frame of mind to do that. I am able to do some work with NBA TV during the season. The folks at Turner ask me to work a couple of nights during the 2014 NCAA tournament. The money is okay, but it isn't enough to cover my gambling habit, not to mention my other expenses. Occasionally, an investment check comes in, and I go right to the OTB.

I opt for early access to my NBA pension. If I wait until I am sixty, that fund will pay me a healthy amount per month for the rest of my life. But I access it at forty-five, which means I get a fraction of what I would have gotten had I waited.

I swim a few times a week to get in something resembling a workout, but I am in the worst shape of my life. Women? No interest. My body is numb, my brain is numb, my spirit is numb. My sex drive is nonexistent.

As if all these areas of my life aren't enough of a mess, I can't get past my troubles with my car registration and driver's license. I get a few tickets for driving with a suspended license, which puts me in nonstop legal purgatory. I park my car backward so the cops won't see that the sticker on my license plate is expired. There is one officer in Phoenix who busts me several times. I get handcuffed, stuffed into a police car, and taken to jail for driving on a suspended license with no insurance.

I ask some friends if I can borrow money. A few of them pony up, including Jim Rome, Jeff Sheppard, and Kevin Vanderpool. Three other buddies, Gus Esposito, Case Clay, and Doug O'Neill, help out as well. I ask Joey Palumbo, a big-time booster at Kentucky, for some cash, but he senses that I'm going in a bad direction, and he smartly refuses.

The NBA TV gig is good for me because it keeps me busy, and I know I need to be somewhat sharp. Once the 2013–14 season ends, I have nothing to do but self-destruct.

I fall behind in my rent. I sleep in my El Camino for two or three days. The car is a disaster—food and wrappers all over the place, pharmacy bags and other shit scattered around. I do whatever I do during the day, then park under a streetlamp at night, handicap the next day's races, and go to sleep. Just lie down in the driver's seat with a blanket and pillow.

I live out of that car a couple of different times. I am worried that someone will show up at my house. I want to disappear.

During my twelve years in the NBA, I made $40 million in salary alone. I was the guy who took care of all my friends and made sure everyone had a good time. We'd go out to dinner and a bar, and I'd pay for everything. I'd drop fifty grand on a group trip to Hawaii. Now I am sleeping in my car, totally out of cash, replaying in my mind every dumbass decision I have ever made over and over and over. I know with absolute confidence my life will never get better. Whoever I had been in the past, this is who I am now, and it is who I am always gonna be.

King Fucking Rex.

● ○ ●

At some point, I realize it is just a matter of time until I will no longer have enough money to buy Suboxone. I need that medicine to keep me from getting sick, so I will have to look for something cheaper. Most times in these situations, the person turns to heroin. Once that line is crossed, it's awfully hard to go back.

In December 2013, I find myself in an Apple Store at a

local mall. The place is packed for the holidays. There are tables set up at the front of the store with some merchandise. People are grabbing boxes, putting them into their shopping bags, and then taking them to the register to pay.

I do the first two steps like everyone else. Then I walk right out without paying. I didn't go in there with the intent to steal, but when I see all that stuff on the table, it seems like an easy thing to do.

I go into a local pawnshop, unload my stuff, and walk out with a few hundred bucks in my pocket. It is pretty easy, so I do it again. And again.

I go back to that same Apple Store several times over the course of seven or eight months. I don't even have enough sense to go to different stores. Ditto for the pawnshop. I go back to the same one, hand over the merchandise, and walk out with cash.

I am in bed on the morning of September 14, 2014, when I am awakened by the doorbell. Zeke answers it. He had transferred to Arizona State following his freshman year at Ball State and is staying with me. He knocks on my bedroom door and tells me a couple of cops are at the house.

"Tell them I'm not here," I say.

Of all the lowlife things I've ever done, asking my own son to lie to the police on my behalf is the lowest. I'm sure the cops know Zeke isn't telling the truth. One of them hands Zeke his card. Zeke hands it to me and leaves for school.

I get dressed, climb into my car, and leave to go get a workout. That's when they nab me.

chapter

15

The hours after I get out of jail are brutal, overwhelming, and very, very frightening. News of my arrest is everywhere. So is my mug shot. I am bombarded by calls and text messages from friends and family, and though I am grateful for the support, I don't want to talk to anyone. I am sure my life is over.

When I spoke with Bridget from the police station, I asked her to get in touch with Gus Esposito, a close friend I had made in Phoenix. Gus connects me with a lawyer, as I knew he would. The next day, I meet the lawyer at his office in downtown Phoenix. He hands me a folder of papers and says, "I'm going to let you take a look at this." Then he leaves the room.

I read through the pages and learn that I am being charged with nine counts of organized retail theft and five counts of trafficking stolen property. The merchandise I stole from the

Apple Store amounts to $14,000. When the lawyer comes back into the room, he tells me the cops have surveillance video showing me swiping the stuff.

"Do you want to watch it?" he asks.

"No," I answer quickly.

I leave it to him to work out all the legal wranglings. There is a very real possibility I am going to have to serve time. My great friends from back home, Mike Ogle and Steve Romines, try to convince me that I need to go back into rehab. Steve is a successful criminal defense attorney, and he thinks it will help my case as well. I know they're right. My sister, Jenny, reaches out to a former Kentucky teammate of mine, Paul Andrews. He is the CFO of the Brook Hospital in Louisville, which specializes in mental health and substance abuse. He arranges to have me admitted right away.

On September 29, two weeks after my arrest, I fly with Jenny to Louisville and check into the Brook. One of the first things they do is weigh me. I tip the scale at 260 pounds, which is by far the heaviest I've ever been and a good 70 pounds above what I weighed when I was in the NBA. My brain is cloudy from the Suboxone, I can't see because my glasses are out of whack, and I have a raging toothache. Other than that, I am in tip-top shape.

They take my phone and personal belongings, and then they lead me to my room. Paul has hooked me up so I don't have to have a roommate, but it is still basically a dorm room—no TV, no nothing, just a bed and a bathroom. When they shut the door and I sit down on the bed, an odd sense of relief washes over me. I am exactly where I need to be.

● ○ ●

The drill is all too familiar. First up is detox. It is a week of hell, but just like before, once I am clean, it is a huge relief. The last thing I want is to see a bunch of people, but I do agree to allow a few visitors. The first person who comes is Keith Vanderpool, my childhood friend and high school teammate from Kentucky. He walks into the room and breaks down. He keeps asking, "What can I do?" I give him nothing. I am still too numb.

A couple of days later, Rick Pitino, who is now the coach at Louisville, comes to see me along with one of his assistants, Vinnie Tatum, who is also a close friend. "How you doing?" he asks.

I start bawling. It is my first real emotional release since all this went down. I keep repeating, "I'm so fucking toxic, my life is over."

Rick has been through some really bad stuff himself, so when he offers advice, he knows what he is talking about. "Over the next couple of years, you're going to eat a lot of shit," he says. "At first, it's going to feel like the size of a beach ball. But if you just do the next right thing, eventually it will be the size of a basketball. If you keep doing the next right thing, it will be the size of a softball. Then a baseball. Then a ping-pong ball. Then it will be a rock and a pebble. It will take some time, but it will happen if you keep doing the next right thing."

My old buddy Kenny Payne, who is an assistant at Kentucky, gets a message to me that he wants to come by with John Calipari, the Wildcats' coach. I appreciate the offer, but I tell him no thanks. Just knowing those guys are willing to visit is enough.

This hospital is in Kentucky, so of course most of the people in here know who I am. The doctors give me an antidepressant for my anxiety. My toothache is getting worse, so Jenny comes and takes me to a dentist. It is an hour-long drive each way, and it is very unnerving. Everything just seems so *loud*—cars, music, voices. The sun makes me squint. If Jenny had dropped me on the side of the road, I would have gone right back to taking drugs. I get the tooth fixed and can't wait to get back to the Brook.

My stomach pain comes back worse than ever. It feels like a knife is cutting up my stomach. It is so bad they actually offer to give me pain medicine, which I refuse to take. They finally have to put me in an ambulance. When I get to the emergency room, the doctor asks for a barium test, where you swallow some dye and they look at it through a scan. It reveals that I have really bad ulcers, which is a common side effect for people who are taking opioids. They send me back to the Brook with some ulcer medication.

By the next day I feel a lot better. The pain is completely gone.

I can't believe it. For twelve years, I have been taking Suboxone to treat that pain. My doctors gave it to me because they thought I was dealing with opiate withdrawal when the whole time I just had a really bad ulcer. The Suboxone was both causing and masking my ulcers. It makes me so angry to think about that.

● ○ ●

Once I get the detox over with, it is time for group therapy. I never took this part seriously during my first stint in rehab, and I avoided it altogether in round two. Now that I am back for a third time, I figure I should do some digging into the factors that led me into this situation. That way, maybe I can avoid having to come back.

Every addict comes with baggage. I have more than my fair share to unpack. For starters, I have to face the anger that had built up over the years about my experiences at Kentucky. I loved playing ball there, but I was still hurt that the people who were closest to me were also telling me who I could and could not date. For all the years I spent in the NBA, I was still known mostly for the two years I played in college. Kentucky basketball was my brand. That anger was something I could not let go of.

I also have a lot of resentment toward my parents for the way they handled me dating Shawn. I have a lot to sort through in general regarding my relationship with my dad. There is also the legacy of my lifelong depression to work through. I have always had that absolute conviction that something shitty was right around the corner. Well, here I am, around that corner, wallowing in shit. I have thought and spoken all of it into existence.

The group sessions are interesting and helpful, but the best thing I do is form a relationship with the private therapist they assign me. Her name is Kim Peabody. We click right away. She says a lot of really smart things, but mostly she has a great demeanor. Whenever I start to go to my dark place, she says, "I promise you, Rex, you're gonna come out of this." People have said that to me before, but for some reason I start to believe her when she says it.

Kim is right by my side for family week. My parents drive in for a meeting. I unload a bunch of thoughts and feelings on them, much of which is directed at my dad. To my surprise, he doesn't resist. Rather, he makes a good-faith effort to listen to what I have to say and acknowledge things he has done. Kim is a tremendous help. When things start heading off the rails, she redirects us.

Jenny participates in these therapy sessions, too. She is shocked to hear how insecure I was all those years. Like everyone else, she just figured the whole time that King Rex was on top of the world.

Next up are my kids. I miss them terribly and want to see them, but I would rather go back to jail than face the four of them. They get there, and we all hug and cry. Zeke, the oldest, seems primarily concerned about me. Caley is affectionate but skeptical, a little standoffish. Tatum keeps asking when

I am coming home and won't let go of my hand. Tyson, my youngest, is about to turn fourteen. She seems to be taking her cues from Caley.

The five of us sit with Kim and talk for a long time. "I'm off this medicine now," I tell them, "and I promise I'm going to do everything I can to stay off it for good."

"What about the gambling?" Caley blurts.

I look over at Kim. Her eyebrow is raised, and she has a smirk on her face.

It's not like I don't realize I have a gambling problem, but my first reaction is to get defensive. *Give me some fucking credit. I just got off these drugs. Do you have any idea what I'm trying to do here?* But it doesn't take long for me to understand that she is right. Of *course* I am a gambling addict. I'm not fooling anyone. This is what therapists call a "moment of clarity," and it is all the more poignant that my daughter forces me to experience it.

That night, we all go out to dinner—me, the kids, and my parents. It is good to feel a little bit normal, if only for a few hours. Then I tell everyone goodbye and promise I'll see them in a few weeks.

I go back to my room, emotionally exhausted and overcome with shame. But I also feel grateful. My kids were a lot easier on me than I would have been on my own parents. For some reason they still love me, despite the hell I am putting them through.

● ○ ●

My sleeping issues get even worse at the Brook. I have so much going on chemically and psychologically, plus it is standard policy for nurses to check on the patients every hour or two throughout the night to make sure they aren't trying to hurt themselves. It's an awful feeling to be tossing and turning all night, knowing the lack of sleep is going to make you feel tired and irritable all the next day.

It takes some time to find the right medicine to help me sleep, but we finally settle on amitriptyline. It doesn't completely fix my insomnia, but it helps. They are also giving me Zoloft. I had tried antidepressants in the past, but Zoloft seems to work the best. It takes a while to kick in, but it doesn't matter because I am so thrilled to be off my Suboxone and not suffering from stomach pain.

There is no exercise room at the Brook, but there is a basketball gym on the property. Actually, it looks more like a dungeon. There is a wood floor and some backboards with rims hanging ten feet high. One day early in my stay, some of us go over there. There are a few basketballs on the floor. I pick one up and shoot it from about twelve feet away. It lands four feet short of the rim.

Someone throws it back to me, and I shoot again. Another airball.

I bend my legs and shoot a third time. The ball grazes the rim. I try to play it off like I am kidding around, but it is fucking pathetic. My muscle memory is completely gone.

Over time, I get a little more functional in the gym. We have a few outdoor Wiffle ball games, too. I whack some home runs and run around the bases acting all silly, getting lost in the moment.

Slowly but surely, I start to feel like a real person again. There are a couple patients who are also former athletes that I bond with. If the three of us aren't in classes together, we are hanging out and eating—and doing a lot of laughing.

I develop a sore throat. The doctors give me some antibiotics, but it doesn't help. Finally, it dawns on me that the reason my throat hurts is because I am laughing so much. It has been so long since I've laughed like that, my body isn't used to it.

I walk down a hallway one day and hear the song "Lovely Day" by Bill Withers playing in the TV room. I stop. I have always loved music, and that is one of my favorite songs. It feels like forever that I have even noticed music. I smile and bob my head to the beat.

As the end of my thirty-day commitment to the Brook approaches, it occurs to me that I have no idea what I am going to do when I get out. That's when I have a visit from John Lucas, who has flown in from Houston. He was an All-American guard at Maryland who was selected with the top pick in the 1976 NBA Draft and played fourteen years in the league. He was also an All-American tennis player in college. I know John well because we were both represented by David Falk. His playing career was derailed by cocaine and alcohol addiction, and ever since then, he has devoted his life to helping other addicts get clean and into recovery. In 1986, he started Athlete Aftercare, a substance-abuse and wellness program in Houston specifically designed for athletes.

Mike Ogle and Steve Romines reached out to John and asked if he would help me. I am real glad to see him. We talk for a while, and I keep telling him how anxious I am to get out of the hospital so I can get home and see my kids.

"When you leave here, you need to come stay with me," he says.

"For how long?"

"As long as it fucking takes."

I resist at first. I am already feeling like the worst father in the world for abandoning my girls. But it doesn't take much to convince me. I have no money, no plan, and nowhere else to go. My kids and my ex-wife are in Phoenix, but there is nothing else for me there, not after all I have been through and what I have just done.

Finally, the day arrives: October 29, 2014. It is time to leave the Brook and start putting my life back together, one bite of shit at a time. Jenny drives me straight to the airport. I thank her for the ride and say goodbye, hoping like hell I will never see the inside of a rehab center again.

chapter
16

John meets me at the Houston airport and drives me to my new home. It is what they call a "sober house," because everyone who lives there is recovering from addictions. Living in a sober house is a way of meeting people who have had similar experiences, and who will hold you accountable while you try to do the same for them.

John's program is highly structured, which is exactly what I need. I am drug tested every day. There are a lot of athletes here. There is plenty of therapy, but I also spend a lot of time in the gym. John trains kids and pros in the Houston area, so there is always someone for us to help work out. I'm in the gym two or three times a day. It is extremely cathartic.

Physically, I feel as good as I have felt in a long time. For the first time in nearly fifteen years, I am not on opioids. My stomach feels great. I don't have any symptoms of withdrawal.

Now all I have to do is learn to function without the drugs. It is almost like learning to walk again. My life has been all about gambling and taking those pills. Before that, it was basketball. Now I have to learn to do without any of these things. It is scary as fuck.

As part of his sobriety, John attends Alcoholics Anonymous meetings every day, sometimes twice a day. I go to almost all of them with him. I never say a word, just sit and listen to everyone's stories. I still don't like all the God talk, but I understand the value of fellowship that comes out of those meetings. Everyone is welcome, everyone is held accountable, and no one is judged.

I'm not in shape to do a whole lot of exercise, but I get into the habit of walking every day. I pop on some headphones and go outside. At first, I can barely walk a mile, but soon I can do more. I'm not eating much, partly because I am trying to lose weight, but largely because I don't have much money to buy food. Every penny counts. I get a licensing check for around twenty grand from the NBA twice a year, as well as a small amount of pension each month. Bridget gets half of whatever I get, and most of the rest goes to pay my legal bills. Whatever is left, I give to the kids.

I have to figure out how to spend idle time. This isn't easy for me. Being with the other guys helps a ton. I feel like I am in a locker room again, enjoying the back-and-forth with the fellas. I think at first that I'll stay only a few weeks, but as I start thinking about my next step, I realize I have nowhere to go. I miss my kids, but Phoenix is not a good option for me, or them, for that matter. I have to fly back a few times to deal with my court case. Each visit reinforces the reality of how dire my situation is.

Even as I am recovering, I am drowning in guilt and shame. I have experienced those feelings in the past, but I always had that magic bullet that I could pop in my mouth and make it all go away. Actually sitting with my emotions, acknowledging and processing them, is a whole new experience. I look back on my life and really come to understand that even when I was young, I was not happy. I'd do dumb shit and get in trouble, and somehow that was fine with me. That set in motion the forces that led to a lot of really bad decisions. I have more clarity than ever, and I hate what I am seeing.

I stay in touch with Kim, my therapist from the Brook, but in Houston I also meet regularly with a counselor named Greg Germany. During one of our sessions those first few days, he says something that sticks with me. I am going on and on about what I have done and why that will make me unemployable for the rest of my life. Greg says, "You know, Rex, there's no reason you can't go out and continue to make a living, in or out of basketball, if you get yourself together and keep yourself together. You're brighter than you give yourself credit for."

One of the mantras you hear all the time in 12 steps is "Do the next right thing." That's what Rick Pitino was referring to when he visited me at the Brook. It's a nice phrase, but it's a lot harder to execute when you've been doing the wrong things for so long. All those bad habits are ingrained in me.

Doing drugs required lying a lot. Even the small, so-called white lies led to bigger ones.

I never realized what a heavy burden it was to keep all those secrets. Now they are all out in the open. I don't want any more.

● ○ ●

The sober house is located in a relatively poor neighborhood of Houston. There are three other guys living with me in the house, one of whom is just a kid, barely eighteen years old. He was doing crack and psychedelics, and his parents had kicked him out. He is so emotionally fragile, it really breaks my heart. Eventually he leaves, and someone else takes his place. Guys continue to cycle in and out throughout my stay.

I get to know the other guys in the program as well. One of them is a seven-foot basketball player. He is talented, but he has a huge drinking problem stemming from the savage beatings he and his brother endured when they were young. That kind of emotional trauma never leaves you. I try to talk to him, but he doesn't communicate real well in English. He is totally lost.

I start to appreciate just how comparatively well off I am. Yes, I had fallen into opioid addiction, but I feel myself coming out of it, and I have plenty of friends who are ready to help me get back on my feet. It makes me feel humble and extremely grateful.

I spend a lot of time in the gym, but I don't play at all. I might shoot a little bit, but my body is all beat up. I won't even go two-on-two half-court. But it is great working out with kids and watching others play. John trains a lot of elite high school prospects around the city, and he takes me with him to watch their games. Fans in the stands recognize me, and they come up to me and give me encouragement.

John also takes me with him on a trip to Oklahoma, where he meets with Sooners coach Lon Kruger and his staff and speaks to their players. I speak to the team as well. Then we drive to Stillwater and do the same thing at Oklahoma State. It feels good to be moving in basketball circles again.

I go to the store, buy some soup, and actually cook it myself. I learn how to do my own goddamn laundry at the age of forty-seven. After two and a half months in that sober house, I am ready to graduate to a place of my own. Except I have no money, so I have to rely on some buddies to pay for me to stay at a Residence Inn in Houston until I can figure out my next move.

Danny Ainge calls me at the hotel one day. He has become the president of the Boston Celtics. "Rex, have you been watching college basketball?" he asks.

I tell him I have.

"Will you write up some reports for us for the draft? We'll pay you five grand." That sounds like five million dollars to me. I tell him I will. When I turn in the reports, he pays me ten grand.

For all the shitty things I've done, I have a lot of really, really great friends, Danny first and foremost. Another is Mark

Verge, who lives in Santa Monica. Mark and I became good friends through our mutual interest in horse racing. He calls me up one day and asks what my plans are post-Houston. I tell him I have none, so he suggests I come hang with him in Los Angeles and see what we can put together. Mark owns a real nice house in Manhattan Beach by the ocean. He offers to pay me a few thousand bucks to live there and take care of it. He also wants me to work with some young local basketball players he knows. All of it sounds pretty good, not least because I'll be able to drive back and forth to Phoenix to see my kids.

I tell John about Mark's proposal. "That sounds like a good idea," he says. "You're ready."

● ○ ●

Mark picks me up at the airport in Los Angeles and takes me to his fabulous house by the water. He rents me a pickup truck, which sticks out in that neighborhood. It is scary being on my own. Nobody tells me what to do or orders me to get tested. If I want to buy drugs or beer or whatever I want, I can do it. I have to learn to wake up every day, establish a proper routine, and find productive ways to fill my time. I get my coffee, go for a long swim, and then walk along the Strand. I continue talking to Kim, but I know I need a local therapist, and I find someone who is really helpful. He is used to dealing with sports and entertainment people.

My court case still hangs over me. I drive my El Camino back and forth to Phoenix to deal with it. The car used to belong to my favorite uncle, E.L. My dad didn't go to most of my games, but E.L. went to every one. I loved that man. That was the car I was driving when I got arrested. It was later impounded, but two of my buddies, Mark Verge and Bryan Freedman, teamed up to buy it back for me. I was touched by that, and insisted I'd pay them back over time. I never have any real fears that I am going back to jail. That is a relief, but it is also another source of guilt. I have spent enough time in the legal system to understand that if you are white and have resources, you can avoid jail time. If you're not white and don't have money, you are probably fucked. The whole thing is such bullshit.

I make no effort to find a full-time job. I assume no one will be interested in me. One thing that gets me through that winter is watching my Kentucky Wildcats finish the regular season undefeated. They win their first four rounds of the NCAA tournament and make the Final Four. The next day, I get a call from Turner Sports, asking if I am interested in calling the Final Four in Indianapolis as part of their Kentucky Teamcast. That's where they show the game on a different network, with a broadcast team of guys who are affiliated with each school. Two executives there, Scooter Vertino and Tara August, were willing to hire me despite what I had done. When I get over the shock of being asked, I say yes.

I arrive at the stadium for the Friday public practice. I am so worried about how people will react to seeing me, but one after another they come up to me, hug me, and offer encouragement. At one point while Duke is practicing, I am walking behind press row and wave at Mike Krzyzewski, the Blue Devils' coach. He motions for me to come onto the court and gives me a hug. He never mentions what I have been through, but I know what he is doing, and I appreciate it greatly. While we are talking, their freshman guard, Grayson Allen, dribbles by, and Coach K says that Grayson reminds him of me a little bit. I guess that is a compliment, because three nights later, Grayson comes off the bench unexpectedly and helps the Blue Devils win the championship.

Aside from my Wildcats losing their Saturday night semifinal to Wisconsin, the weekend is an amazing experience. For me to think about where I have been to where I am at that moment, it seems like a miracle. Basketball is saving me—again.

● ○ ●

Until I got to California, I never quite realized how much of my life had been consumed by the need to acquire opioids. The previous fifteen years was a never-ending blur of trips to the doctor's office, dealing with pharmacies, working through all the hassles that go with maintaining a string of lies that enabled me to get my fix. And that's not including all the drug dealers I had to go through. Drug dealers aren't, like, the most *reliable* people on the planet. I truly believe all of that is behind me, especially since I am living without stomach pain.

I take advantage of the scenery to go on long walks. I can't go very far at first, but eventually my legs start coming back.

My kids take turns visiting me over the summer. When I saw them in Phoenix, I hardly had any money to feed them, much less do fun stuff together. Now I have this big, beautiful house by the ocean. We can go to the beach or walk on the Strand or go into downtown Hermosa or Manhattan Beach and get some ice cream. I feel like a real dad for the first time in a long time.

In California, medical marijuana has become a lot more commonplace. I was never much interested in pot, but the more I read up on it, the more interested I get. I especially like that you can inhale it from a vape pen. I don't want to inhale smoke, and I don't want to smell like weed. The pen solves both those problems.

There are two basic strains of marijuana: indica and sativa. Indica mellows you out and helps you fall asleep. Sativa gives you more creative energy and a sense of euphoria. I get a prescription for sativa and buy a pen. I take a couple of tugs, sit for a few minutes . . . and feel better almost instantly. Not freaky high or anything like that. Just a little bit happier. I am able to sit and watch a TV show for thirty minutes without having to get up a bunch of times. My thoughts seem a little more organized. My worries are a little less worrisome.

It isn't long before marijuana is a daily habit. I discuss this with Kim as well as my therapist in LA. Both of them warn me of the dangers of going down this road, but neither tries to talk me out of it. As long as I am open about it, they give their blessings.

Being so open about my life is a new experience. I take it a step further that summer by agreeing to do a series of interviews with *Sports Illustrated*. I'm not fully truthful with the reporter, especially when discussing my finances, but for the most part, I do lay out the gory details of what I have been through. When the story is published in July, I go into a panic. I don't read the article, but lots of people reach out to say that they love it. It is another healthy reminder that I have a lot of folks who care about me, that we live in a forgiving society, and that I have a chance at a decent future if I can just keep my shit together.

One of the coolest offshoots of that story is that I am invited to speak to local groups about my experiences. This is another big step forward. I've gone from believing I am permanently toxic to realizing I can use my mistakes to encourage and inspire others. Turns out that the best cure for self-pity is to become selfless. In helping others, I help myself most of all.

● ○ ●

After a few months at Mark's house, I feel like I am wearing out my welcome. He encourages me to stay, but there are times when he and his family want to use the house and I have to clear out. I move into a small guest cottage behind a house in Santa Monica owned by Brian Freedman, a top entertainment lawyer. I've been training Brian's son, Spencer, and I'm very appreciative that he is letting me stay there while I ponder my next move.

Money is real tight, but I get a financial boost when Leah Wilcox, a VP at the NBA who is the league's liaison to former players, reaches out to let me know about a program the league has established to assist former players who have fallen on hard times. It gives me access to roughly $30,000, which I can withdraw from in small increments. I have a steady stream of families with young kids who play basketball, and they pay me to work their sons out and give 'em some pointers. I make around five hundred bucks a week doing these sessions. I take whatever money I have and go to the grocery store, and I can buy just enough gas to get to where I need to go. Whatever is left over goes to my kids and my lawyers.

I almost never get recognized walking around LA, but when I go into a gym, there are usually people who know who I am. I'm sure a lot of 'em know I had been arrested, but nobody says anything. It is good for my mindset to do these workouts. I have gotten to the point where I can get out there, move around a little, and work up a sweat. My shooting touch has returned somewhat, and once in a while, I get up there and half dunk it.

By this time, I have become really close with Josh Hopkins, an actor from Lexington who has done a bunch of TV shows and movies. Josh's message offering his support was the first text message I read when the cops handed me my phone in that jail cell. I barely knew him, but that's the kind of man he is. When I tell Josh that I am looking for a place to live, he says that he is headed to Prague at the end of the year to shoot a movie, and that I am welcome to stay in his empty house in Sherman Oaks. Once again, I am on the move.

I know I need to exert myself every day, for mental reasons as much as physical ones. There is a hiking trail up a mountain near Josh's house, and no matter what, I force myself to get up early, have a cup of coffee, and walk up that mountain. Zeke moves in with me, and sometimes it is so hot I damn near pass out and have to call and ask him to come get me. If I go two or three days without working out, I don't feel right. As long as I keep moving, I have a chance to get through the day. Josh eventually comes back from Prague, and the three of us live together in his house. Josh and I are so much alike it's kind of scary, but mostly comforting.

My case is finally settled in September, when I am sentenced to probation and agree to pay back $15,000 to the Apple Store. As part of my probation, I am required to serve hundreds of hours of community service, so fulfilling that obligation helps keep me busy. I visit nonprofit programs all over Southern California and talk to their kids. I tell my story over and over again. Josh eventually comes back from Prague, and the three of us live together in his house. Josh and I are so much alike it's kind of scary, but mostly comforting.

I am acutely aware of just how fortunate I am that, unlike most people who are in my situation, I have people in my life who can help with my finances. My cousin Kristina, who almost won the Miss USA pageant, helps me pay about $75,000 worth of legal bills and other debts. It takes me about seven years, but I manage to pay it back. My buddy

Gus from Phoenix helps me out, too. Without them and a few others being so generous, I don't know what I would do. I am also lucky that the NBA recently set up a system so that all their retired players can have health insurance for the rest of their lives. For a long time, I didn't want to go to a doctor or a dentist because I didn't have insurance. Now I can.

Even with all this help, I am living meal to meal. It sucks when your credit is so fucked that you have to pay for everything with cash. I can't even open a bank account. I go in to try it, but I still have accounts in various places I had opened as a way to hide gambling money from Bridget, and I still owe money on some of them.

In the fall of 2016, I get a call from DeWayne Peevy, who is an assistant athletic director for communications at Kentucky. DeWayne asks if I have any interest in doing some radio coverage of UK basketball. "Absolutely," I reply. Whatever misgivings I may have—ambivalence about my relationship with the fans, shame over the embarrassment I had caused the program with my shoplifting arrest—are swept aside by the harsh reality that I need cash, and nobody else is calling. I don't even ask DeWayne what they are paying.

DeWayne says he will report our conversation to Paul Archey, who is the head of JMI Sports, a media company in Lexington that produces the UK radio broadcasts and who had asked DeWayne to reach out. Paul calls and gives me the offer: a whopping 125 bucks a game. I say yes.

I have been through a lot of sharp turns in my life, but

this is one twist I never see coming. After everything I have been through, after all the success and fame, embarrassment and pain, after all the ups and downs of trying to live up to being King Rex and then being exposed for who I really was, after holding on to all that anger about where I was raised and who I was surrounded by and the attitudes of people who lived there, I am going to try to get reborn in the place where it all started, the place where they knew me best and hurt me most: my old Kentucky home.

Ain't that a bitch.

chapter
17

I have no place of my own in Lexington, and I certainly am not going to stay with my parents. So I move in with Jenny. This is very kind of her considering I can't help out with rent or other household expenses. Her husband works in Louisville, and I am able to drive her daughter to school occasionally and do other stuff.

It is an awkward situation. There has always been tension between us, and now we are under the same roof for the first time since high school. I'm sure I grate on her.

About six months into my stay, Jenny and I get in some kind of argument. "Well, maybe you shouldn't be living here then," she says. I decide she is right. I check into a cheap motel and stay there for three months. Then I rent a condo that my cousin Kristina bought so I could rent it from her.

It is weird being back in Lexington again, but it feels good, too. Lexington is home. It's where I had a lot of great memories and formative experiences. Some of my best friends are here. I feel relieved that I don't have to hide who I am anymore. King Rex is dead and gone. If someone wants to be my friend or not, that is up to them, but at least everyone knows the deal.

To my surprise, there is not a single moment where I feel judged. If anything, people are sympathetic. Kentucky is ground zero for the opioid crisis in America, along with Ohio and West Virginia. These are states with a lot of manual laborers, especially coal miners and factory workers, and the vultures at the pharmaceutical companies recognized them as easy marks. They also got plenty of help from politicians whose palms they greased. People in these states are hurting all the time, but they need to work, so hey, how about taking this little pill and making the pain go away?

I get invitations from all over the state to speak about my experiences with opioids. Patrick Gaunce, an old friend from Kentucky who's been helping me out, sets up a lot of the visits. Sometimes I get paid 500 bucks or so, but I do a bunch of 'em for free. I visit a lot of rehab facilities. If I am heading someplace to do a paid gig, I might call one or two spots along the way and ask if I can come by and say hello. I drive to these remote, rural towns and try to cheer people up. I share my story—again—and listen to them talk about their problems. Lots of times we just talk basketball. It is enough for me to give them something to smile about for an hour or two. I know firsthand how much rehab sucks.

When I was at the Brook, I got to be friendly with a fellow patient who was a huge Louisville fan. I promised her that when we got out of the hospital, I would take her to a Louisville game and give her the VIP treatment. Sure enough, she calls me, and I fulfill my promise. She doesn't stop smiling all night.

I am walking into my local gym one day wearing headphones, not wanting to talk to anybody. When I check in, this kid behind the counter says to me, "Are you Rex?"

"Yeah," I say quickly, and go to work out.

He stops me as I'm leaving. He is young, maybe twenty-five years old. "Mr. Chapman, I'm sorry to bother you," he says. "You spoke about six months ago at a rehab place where my dad was staying. He really took what you said to heart. He's been out now about six months, he's clean, and he's never been so happy. I just wanted to thank you."

I feel like such an asshole for how I had acted. I have tears in my eyes as I grab the kid, hug him, and say, "Thank you for telling me that. That's amazing."

● ○ ●

The best part about being back in Kentucky is getting to be around the team again. I watch practices, go out to dinner with Kenny Payne and some other buddies, and soak in the excitement of the games. There's nothing like Rupp Arena.

John Calipari is about to begin his eighth season as coach. I first met Cal when I was in high school attending Five-Star Basketball Camp. He was a young, up-and-coming coach who had a ton of energy and a bright future. I played against Cal's teams when he was coaching the New Jersey Nets, and when he was at Memphis and I was working in the NBA, I used to call him once in a while to ask him about his players. On the morning of Calipari's press conference at Kentucky, he called a bunch of former players, and I was one of them. When he asked if I had any advice, I told him that Kentucky's longtime legendary equipment manager, Bill Keightley, had just died, and it might be nice if he offered condolences to Bill's wife, Hazel.

A few hours later, I was watching the press conference, and sure enough, Hazel was sitting right there at the table with Cal. He gave me credit for making the suggestion. He didn't have to mention me, but recognizing Bill was a great move on his part.

I know I wouldn't be working for JMI Sports if Cal hadn't given his okay. That is very generous, because two years before, I had done something real shitty to him. It happened the night Kentucky played UConn in the 2014 NCAA championship game. I was covering the Final Four for Turner, and when I got to the stadium, a close buddy of Cal's told me that the Lakers were likely hiring him. I was still on the Suboxone and not thinking clearly, so I sent out a message on Twitter saying that, win or lose, it was "a #DoneDeal" that Cal was going to coach the Lakers. Setting aside that it was a horrendous use of a hashtag, there was no basis for me to report that with such certainty. It caused a disruption on a night when all of Big Blue Nation should have been focused on the game.

I had originally set up a Twitter account at the suggestion of Jim Rome, the highly successful sports radio personality who had become a good friend. I went on Jim's show a bunch of times, and he used to give me shit about thoroughbred racing. Eventually, he got interested and started buying up racehorses. He visited Lexington—he called it "Lex Vegas," which I thought was brilliant—in the summer of 2010. I took him to racetracks and thoroughbred farms so he could learn more about the business. At one point during the trip, Jim started talking about Twitter, which had launched in 2006. "You really should be on it," he said. I set up an account, and within a couple of hours I had about fifty thousand followers. I didn't tweet often. When I did, it was usually to bait people into having stupid arguments about basketball.

My tweet about Calipari caused a big stir, and I foolishly went on Twitter to defend it. After the game, which Kentucky lost, Calipari was asked about it. He was already bummed that his team had lost the game, and now he had to answer for my stupidity. "I'm not going to even dignify that stuff," he said. Needless to say, he never went to the Lakers.

When I went back to Lexington to play a charity softball game in the summer of 2016, I texted Cal and asked if I could come see him. I sat in his office and apologized for my tweet. Cal laughed and said, "What tweet? I don't even know what you're talking about. Forget about it." He was a lot more gracious than I probably would have been if I were sitting in his chair.

My job with JMI is a pretty light lift. My duties are limited to pregame and postgame shows. We almost never travel to road games. I don't consider myself a great broadcaster, but I have done enough of it to feel confident that I will at least not embarrass myself too badly. The job makes me feel valued again. UK asks me to make an unpaid appearance once in a while on the school's behalf, and I am happy to do it.

The Suns hire me to be a consultant. I fly to Phoenix for some meetings, get to know their players, scout college games, whatever the team needs.

My friends at Turner also invite me to Atlanta to do some studio appearances for NBA TV. Every single person I work with at Turner is absolutely aces. I'm not just talking about the on-air talent or top executives. I'm talking about the camera folks, sound technicians, researchers, producers, makeup artists—everyone. They represent every race, ethnicity, gender, religion, and sexual orientation there is. It's what America should be about.

I also pick up work doing radio with a company based in San Francisco called TuneIn. I am on air with them during the NBA playoffs from a studio in Lexington, and then travel to Cleveland and Golden State for the Finals. I'm not making a ton of money, but I don't *need* a ton of money. I chased cash for so long, not so much because I needed or wanted it, but almost as a competitive thing. But now, without the need to buy drugs or gamble, I don't have a big monthly nut. My biggest financial stress is paying off my lawyers and other debts. I'm not living the high life by any stretch, but I am making ends meet, and for the most part, I am mentally and physically healthy. All this is new for me, and quite the welcome change.

● ○ ●

Something else happens in the fall of 2016 that changes me—and America—forever. Donald Trump gets elected president.

The idea that an election would have such an impact on me would have seemed laughable to my old teachers. Until then, I showed very little interest in history, current events, or anything that didn't have to do with basketball. What did I need that for? We talked about what was going on in the world in my house, but my parents and I rarely had political conversations. I never served jury duty, either. If I got a summons while I was in the NBA, I'd hand it over to some team official, and the obligation would disappear.

I met Trump one time. I was playing against the Knicks at Madison Square Garden, and Trump rode the freight elevator after the game with a bunch of players. His girlfriend at the time, Marla Maples, was with him, and Trump wouldn't make eye contact with any of us. He had a worried look seeing her surrounded by all those young athletes. That was my impression, anyway.

I only paid half attention to the 2016 presidential campaign. I was trying to get my own life together. But I saw enough to know that Trump was a con man. I knew there were a lot of racists in this world, but I had a hard time believing any of them would get fooled into believing this guy gave a fuck about them. Trump never hung out with a working stiff in his entire life. He was born into wealth and spent all his time trying to prove he belonged in the company of the rich and famous. Which was fine—but don't turn around and tell me he's representing America's working class. He was not representing them, he was *using* them. Not to mention all the racist shit he was peddling: the Central Park Five bullshit, the Obama birther lies. I really thought as a country that we were past most of that stuff.

Now he has won. I am fucking blown away.

It is hard for me to understand what has just happened, so I start to pay more attention to what is going on. When I go to the gym or the YMCA to work out, all the TVs are tuned to Fox News. Even when I watch the local news, I hear stuff that I know isn't true.

True to my ADD nature, I go from being disinterested to being hyperfocused. I watch cable news for hours, read everything I can, and talk to people who are smarter than me about this stuff (which isn't hard to find). I bring to all this an innate understanding of the media that I developed during all those years playing and dealing with reporters. I know firsthand that much of what is reported in the press is wrong. When I read something or see someone talking on TV, I don't just take what they are saying at face value. I try to find out who they are, what else they have written or said, who they work for, and what their angle might be.

I reach a boiling point in the fall of 2017 when Trump goes after Colin Kaepernick. Colin is an NFL quarterback who had taken the San Francisco 49ers to the Super Bowl, but at the beginning of the 2016 season, he started kneeling during the pregame national anthem as a way of bringing attention to racial inequalities in our criminal justice system. Many people interpreted this as Colin protesting the national anthem, but that's not what he was really doing. They also said he was disrespecting our military, when in fact he got the idea to kneel from a retired Green Beret and former NFL player named Nate Boyer, who thought that it was a more respectful way to make his point than sitting down.

I respect the hell out of Colin for putting himself out there, knowing it could jeopardize his playing career. I certainly never had the balls to do that when my coaches at Kentucky were telling me who I could and could not date. Whatever anyone thinks about what Colin is doing, I hope—and frankly assume—that everyone can at least respect him for exercising his First Amendment rights. Isn't that what the flag is supposed to represent?

I also know that for a white guy like me, there is no way to truly understand what it is like to be Black in America. There is also no denying that Blacks are getting a raw deal in our justice system, and that they are disproportionately mistreated badly by police. That's just a fucking fact.

We tend not to expect much from our presidents, but we do expect them to try to help bring us together around race. Trump, however, goes the opposite way. He sees a spark of anger and pours gasoline on it, all because he believes that if Blacks and whites are arguing with each other, then it will benefit him politically. He says that NFL owners should "fire" players who refuse to stand for the anthem and calls the players who are protesting "sons of bitches." Not only that, but at the same time Trump is going after Kaepernick, he is praising NASCAR and its fans. How fucking blatantly racist can you get?

It is as if all the stupidity and bigotry that I have witnessed and then suppressed all my life boils back up and explodes out of the top of my head. I simply cannot believe that we have an open, unapologetic racist as our president. Not only that, all those Republicans who had called him out for it before the election—remember when Lindsey Graham called Trump a "xenophobic bigot"?—are falling in line like cowards. I think about Mitch McConnell's top guy showing off his Confederate flag sticker like it was normal back when I was in high school, and I realize that this racist outreach to white voters has been going on for a long time.

The Kaepernick episode pushes me from profound concern to raw anger. I have a lot of knowledge I didn't have before and a fresh set of opinions. I don't know what to do with these notions, so I start putting them out on Twitter. My sense of humor fits right in with the spirit of Twitter. I have a knack for squeezing my thoughts into that tight space while keeping them sharp. I'm not sure what I am accomplishing, but it feels good to do it.

All this is so new to me that I don't even realize I am being ideological. One day a buddy of mine who shares my point of view says to me, "I never knew you were a liberal snowflake." I never knew it, either, but I guess the description fits.

In late 2017, I get a call from a UK alum asking if I would be willing to speak at a meeting of the National Safety Council in Chicago about opioids. I say yes, and the appearance goes over well. A short while later, I get another call from the council inviting me to accompany a delegation to the White House to do an appearance with President Trump. I am adamant at first that I won't do it, but some friends make a convincing case that I can help a lot of people by going. So I tell the folks at the council that I am willing to do it.

A few weeks later, I get a call disinviting me to the event. Apparently, they sent a list of attendees to the White House and were told that if I was included, then nobody from the council could come. I bow out.

● ○ ●

Nobody at JMI comes right out and tells me to stop tweeting about politics, but I can tell it is becoming a problem for them. Clearly, the vast majority of Kentucky's fan base disagrees with my point of view. I don't care much about that, but as a media company we have to be careful about pissing off our audience with stuff that has nothing to do with basketball. The last thing I want is to put JMI in a bad spot. They took a chance on a thief and a drug addict. And if I'm being honest, I am just starting to get back into a position where I can make a living again. I don't want to piss off our audience too much, either.

Still, some things are creeping up that give me flashbacks. For example, there are two seniors on that first Kentucky team I cover who are good reserves. One is Derek Willis, a six-foot-nine forward, and the other is Dominique Hawkins, a six-foot guard. Both add value, but when I am on the radio taking calls from Kentucky fans, I hear a ton of people wondering why Derek isn't playing more, and very few saying the same thing about Dominique. Dominique is Black, and Derek is white. (Well, at least he looks white. He is half Native American.) Maybe I am overthinking things, but that seems awfully suspicious, especially since I think Dominique is clearly the better player.

I have an even stronger response when I see the fan reaction to Tyler Herro, a six-foot-five white guard from Milwaukee. Tyler is quick and bouncy, and he is a natural scorer. He is the lowest-ranked of our five recruits, so people aren't expecting him to be as good as he is out of the gate. Tyler isn't a Kentucky kid, but immediately everyone says he is "another Rex Chapman." That really bothers me. There are plenty of past Kentucky guards who could run, jump, and score a ton of points. Tyler plays more like Devin Booker than me. Yet, because he and I are both white, I am the obvious comparison.

That doesn't seem to bother Tyler. In fact, when they have a dunk contest at Midnight Madness, DeWayne Peevy calls me up and asks if Tyler can wear my jersey. I say sure and give it to him to use for the contest.

I finally decide to do something about it. I speak with a writer at the *Athletic*, a brand-new national sports platform, and we craft what I think is a rather tame, nuanced column under my byline pointing out this pattern of comparing white players to white players and Black players to Black ones and asking people to think more deeply about it. I don't call anyone a racist. I just describe what is happening, and I touch on my own frustrations at being compared to Kyle Macy, when in reality I played more like Darrell Griffith.

Before we publish the column, I show it to some friends. They think it is terrific. Then I show it to my colleagues at JMI. They do not think it is so terrific. Once again, no one tells me I can't publish it, but it is clear that doing so will make things difficult for them, and by extension, for me. So I do what I have always done when it comes to this stuff: I fold. The piece never runs.

chapter

18

One day in January 2019, I am sitting at home in Lexington, spending way too much time on my phone, as usual. I stumble on a video of a guy standing on a paddleboard in the ocean. A school of dolphins is heading his way. One of the dolphins jumps out of the water and knocks him clear off his board.

I burst out laughing. I think to myself, *That's a fucking charge.*

I post the video on Twitter and put a three-word question above it: Block or charge?

The tweet gets a lot of response. I don't think much of it at first, but over the next few days, I am flooded with videos showing all kinds of unintentional collisions. A girl riding her bike into a signpost. A dude jumping off a roof into a pool and half landing on cement. A kid skateboarding down a handrail and landing on his balls.

I retweet the videos with the same comment on top: Block or charge?

My follower count skyrockets. People flood my direct messages with videos, and not just of collisions, either. Some are of the feel-good variety. I am especially partial to dog videos. I post them with the simple tagline "Dogs bruh."

My favorites are the heart tuggers. An autistic kid making a free throw and being mobbed by his teammates. A deaf girl hearing for the first time. A nurse who helped a young girl recover from a spinal cord injury melting into tears when she sees her former patient jump out of her wheelchair. I post these videos and write above them, "This is the Twitter content I'm here for."

I add followers by the thousands. People ask me where I am finding the videos, but the truth is, the videos are finding me. They come from literally all over the world. There is one guy named Sander van den Berg who lives in the Netherlands. His stuff is great. When we first connect, he has just a few followers, but eventually I help him get over two million and pay him 500 bucks a month to send me content. The trouble isn't finding videos, it's deciding which ones to post. Meanwhile, I am making friends with people I have never met or even spoken to, many of whom are famous and have huge followings of their own.

I tweet and tweet and tweet. It's not like I have a full-time job or lots of hobbies. I'm sure it isn't the healthiest habit, but it is better than blowing thousands at the racetrack. There's not a lot of tenderness on Twitter. It's mostly anger, hate, and ignorance, posted by keyboard warriors who would never say shit to the person face-to-face. I like knowing I am giving people a brief chuckle during what otherwise might be a real stressful day.

I know things are officially out of hand when my buddy Craig Wadler texts a link to a CNN story that includes a tweet I had posted. "You're ubiquitous," he writes. I have to look the word up.

In the summer of 2019, I travel to Chicago to attend the NBA's scouting combine for that year's draft. I am standing by the court when a young prospect named Grant Williams walks by. Grant is an outstanding player at Tennessee, and he will soon be picked in the first round by the Boston Celtics.

As Grant walks past, he glances at the pass hanging around my neck. He stops when he reads my name.

"Rex Chapman?" he asks. "The Twitter Guy?"

I bust out laughing. "Yup, that's me. Best of luck this week."

If there's one place you'd think I'd be recognized for being a former NBA player, it would be at an official NBA event. I was an All-American in high school and at the University of Kentucky, a first-round draft pick who played in the league for twelve years. I scored nearly ten thousand points in the NBA and made an All-Star team. Grant Williams didn't know any of that. He only knew me as the Twitter Guy.

I wait for all of it to flame out, but instead it burns hotter. I get a call from a guy named Matt Harrigan who runs a media company called Adult Swim that produces streaming shows. He is close with David Helmers, one of my Fellas from Kentucky, and he suggests the two of us host a show called *Block or Charge?* The premise is that David and I watch these videos, crack jokes about 'em, and then debate whether they are blocks or charges. The producers find the videos for us. All we have to do is riff. We do about thirty episodes and get paid a few grand a month. It is easy money.

● ○ ●

As my following grows, I have to check myself. I have just started to drift into a comfortable obscurity. Do I really want to disrupt that balance and raise my profile again? Do I want to put myself out there, even if it is through silly videos? What is the point of all this anyway?

My answer comes on May 25, 2020.

That is the day George Floyd is murdered by a policeman in broad daylight in Minneapolis. The video of Floyd's murder goes viral that night. It shocks the world, and it strikes a major chord in me. I can't believe what I am seeing—and yet, it is eminently believable. Everyone knows—or should know—that Blacks are treated way worse than whites by police and the justice system. That's just a given. I have been in enough cars that got pulled over by cops to understand how different the reactions are. My white buddies think it is funny. The Black guys are scared out of their minds.

I know that as a white man I can never, ever truly understand what it means to be Black in this country. Yet, I have experienced racism at a level very few white people have. I have so much resentment that built up over time about the people I felt did me wrong because I had a Black girlfriend— my parents, my coaches, the fans in Kentucky, people around the NBA. I haven't quite realized the extent to which that anger has been bubbling up. I am like a volcano, with all that hot lava building and building and building. When I see the video of George Floyd's murder, I erupt.

But what can I even do about it besides tweet incessantly? The country has been locked down for nearly three months because of the COVID-19 pandemic. We are in scary, scary times. The NCAA tournament has been canceled, and all the sports leagues have suspended competition. In times like these, you look to your leaders for guidance and encouragement, but President Trump acts like a buffoon day in and day out. At first, he said it was just a couple of sick people from China. Then he said the pandemic would go away like magic. Then he said we'd be open again by Easter. He said everyone who wanted a test could get one, which was a lie. He bragged about the TV ratings for his briefings. I thought, "Fuck, man, people aren't watching to see you, they're watching because they're fucking *scared.*"

Once the Floyd video gets out, people start taking to the streets in protest, pandemic be damned. Tensions are running high all around. As usual, Trump takes the most racist stance he can. He has people gassed who are peacefully protesting outside the White House. (We'll find out later he had asked some of his advisors if they could order police to shoot at them.) Then he walks across the street to stage a photo op in front of a church he has never prayed in and holds up a Bible he has never read.

Like so many Americans, I sit at home, quarantining from the virus, watching it unfold with disgust. The difference is, I have a platform now. I am a former professional athlete and a *social media influencer*, whatever that means. All my life, I have chickened out because I was afraid of losing everything. But as the Bob Dylan lyric goes, "When you got nothin', you got nothin' to lose." It is time to make myself heard.

I open up my laptop and write a rough draft of a column. I send it to a couple of friends, Sam Youngman and Randi Mayem-Singer, who are accomplished writers and help me organize my thoughts. Sam has also been helping me make smart political comments on Twitter. Once I feel the column is ready, I email it to Jerry Tipton, the longtime UK beat writer at the *Lexington Herald-Leader*. I tell Jerry I don't care where the paper puts the column, but that if they are going to use it, they have to use all of it.

Jerry passes it along to his bosses. On June 9, 2020, the piece runs under the headline "'Injustice, Double Standards and Heartbreaking Bigotry.' Rex Chapman on Race in America." The article runs not in the sports section but in the news section. It marks the first time I have publicly described my encounters with racism while I was playing for the Wildcats:

I never understood why my dating habits were such a difficult topic for people when I was younger. It made no sense to me. I grew up listening to hip-hop. My upbringing was infused with black culture. Black athletes and entertainers were emulated all around me—so why was I discouraged from dating or loving a woman of color? Why is that?

I went to parties in the suburbs "country" where I grew up as a teenager in a town of about 50,000 people. I also went to those same parties in the projects. Because I came up in both places. And in both locations, underage kids were drinking, smoking weed, basically just behaving like teenagers. But I'll give it to you straight: When the cops pull up to a bonfire out in the country, the kids don't move a muscle. Because they all know nobody is going to jail. When your parents likely know the sheriff, the prosecutor or the judge, your mom and dad get called. You get in "trouble" at home. On the other hand, when cops pull up to a party in the projects, people run and scatter because they know they're going to jail. They know they're getting fined, beat-up, or even shot. I saw that difference firsthand.

For once, I'm not the slightest bit worried about how anyone, much less Kentucky fans, will react. I use my expansive Twitter following to push the piece out.

In a flash, it is everywhere. I get a message over Twitter from Stephanie Ruhle, an anchor at MSNBC, asking me to come on her show to discuss the piece. Since we are in a pandemic, there is no need to go to a studio. I can just do the interview from my home computer.

Stephanie asks what made me decide to write the column. I start to tell the story of the fan at my high school game who praised me because "you get to be white." I barely get through it without breaking down.

"I'm tired of holding this stuff back," I say, gathering myself. "I was a lottery pick in the NBA, and since then I've lived in my car. I didn't say a lot of this stuff when I was younger, I think, because I was a little concerned about how it might affect my pocketbook. I'm not concerned about that anymore. I can go back and live in my car again. I'm gonna be honest about this stuff, and if fewer opportunities come my way because of speaking out for things I know are just, then so be it."

After all those years of holding my tongue, I am finally starting to find my voice.

● ○ ●

When I first posted that dolphin video, I had around eighty thousand followers on Twitter. A year later, it is over a million. I am retweeted by, and exchange direct messages with, some of the biggest personalities you can think of. Many of the relationships jump to text messages and phone calls. Hell, Donald Trump even retweets one of my videos, not knowing that I have been shredding him for years.

A podcasting company reaches out to my agent and asks if I want to host my own show. I say yes but also want Josh Hopkins, my Kentucky buddy and actor, to host it with me.

The result is *The Rex Chapman Show with Josh Hopkins*. Josh and I love doing it. We develop a running gag on every episode called "Book Club." It goes like this:

"Okay, Josh, before we get to today's guest, it's time for Book Club. Did you read anything this week?"

"Y'know, Rex, I was kind of busy this week, so no, I didn't read anything. What about you?"

"Well, I actually wasn't that busy. I thought about reading something, but then I decided I'd rather not."

"And that's been Book Club."

Because of all of my relationships, both in sports and on Twitter, we have a terrific lineup of guests. I am surprised at how much I enjoy doing the research and coming up with questions. I am always nervous that I might sound stupid, but that only makes me work extra hard to prepare.

Around the same time, Steve Nash calls and asks if I want to do some podcasting with his production company. His idea is to do a show called *Charges*, where I interview people who have gone through experiences like mine with respect to addiction, crime, and other mental health challenges. As we are developing the show, we have a conversation about what the cover art should be. We go back and forth on some different options. I finally say, "Let's just use my mug shot." I think the producers may have wanted to do that all along but were afraid to ask.

For so long I have been ashamed of that picture. If you google "Rex Chapman," that's usually the first thing that comes up. Using that picture is my way of taking away its power over me. It is the same attitude I had when I started going bald. Yeah, it sucks, but as long as I can't get rid of it, I might as well own it. The title track each week features the sounds of TV anchors announcing the news of my arrest. I am really putting it out there—and I am okay with it. That is progress, I guess.

Unlike the other show, where the guests are often good friends of mine or connected to the NBA, the people who come on *Charges* are usually people I have never spoken to before. I do my research and think real hard about what I want to ask. I find some nugget from the person's past, and then ask him or her about it. I have been on the other side of this enough times to know that it sucks when you feel like the person asking the questions hasn't done his or her homework. These people don't have to come on my show. I want them to know that I respect their time.

After I have done a bunch of episodes, I take a trip out of town and board my dog in a local kennel. When I get back to Lexington, I go to pick him up. An older woman recognizes me and approaches. I assume she wants to talk about Kentucky basketball. Instead, she wants to talk about her son. "He was arrested a few weeks ago," she says as tears come to her eyes. "He's been in and out of rehab. I've been listening to your podcast, and it gives me hope."

I hug her and wish her son the best. Like Andy Dufresne says in *The Shawshank Redemption*, hope is a good thing, maybe the best of things. Knowing I gave a total stranger a little hope makes me feel really good. I am gratified to know that something worthwhile is coming out of all the shit I have been through.

* ○ *

Zeke has been living with me in Lexington, where he coaches freshman and JV basketball at Sayre School, a local private school. He is great at it. Everyone at the school loves him, especially the players and their parents. I've never met anybody who doesn't like Zeke.

After a while, I realize that Zeke is living with me partly because he is worried I will go off the rails again. When Steve Nash gets hired to be the head coach of the Brooklyn Nets in the fall of 2020, he calls to tell me that he has a spot for Zeke on his video staff if he wants it. Zeke jumps at the chance. In November, Zeke and I pack up the car and drive to New York. We have a great few days together. We go to lunch with Steve and his wife, and then we spend a few days looking for an apartment. We find him a great place, get him all set up, and he goes to his first day of work.

Eventually, the time is approaching for me to say goodbye. I am dreading it. I'm not good when it comes to dealing with these kinds of feelings. I usually run from them, and Zeke does, too.

He calls me up and asks, "When are you planning on leaving?"

"I think I'm gonna go right now," I reply. I want to get this over with.

I call the front desk to ask them to bring my car around. I step outside. It is foggy and rainy. The valet pulls up in my car. I climb inside, put my home address in the navigator, and turn on the radio.

And what song comes on first? "Cat's in the Cradle," by Harry Chapin. I sob as I head for home.

chapter
19

Between my podcasting work and my presence on Twitter, I become increasingly outspoken about politics and current events, much to the chagrin of many of my friends. I have become one of the faces of America's opioid epidemic, which leads me to be interviewed on various talk shows and podcasts. I'll venture to say there's not a single person in Kentucky who hasn't been impacted by opioids one way or another. Either they've been addicted, or someone close to them has, or someone close to them has had someone close to them get addicted or die. It doesn't take a whole lot of degrees of separation. There are a couple of times when I am driving around and come upon a car at a stoplight that isn't moving. The person behind the wheel is out cold—dead or dying, I can't tell. I call 911.

It pisses me off that not only are our political leaders not doing anything about it, but instead they are invested in protecting the pharmaceutical companies that profit off of it. The worst offender is Mitch McConnell, who has consistently fought any kind of positive change to the health care system while taking a whole bunch of money from Big Pharma. Mitch has been in the Senate since I was in high school. It is unfathomable to me that anyone in Kentucky would want him to be there this long.

Then there's our other US senator, that great patriot, Rand Paul. Just two weeks after George Floyd's murder, Rand was the only senator to oppose the Emmett Till Antilynching Act. Think about that. If you're anti anti-lynching, doesn't that make you *pro* lynching? Rand said it was because the bill's definition of lynching was too broad, but I recognized it for what it was: a blatant dog whistle to appeal to the most backward-thinking racists in our state. Fucking despicable.

I continue to tweet out funny and endearing videos, but these are serious times. If something bothers me, I feel compelled to weigh in. Sadly, there is no shortage of reasons to be pissed off. In January 2021, for example, a bunch of Kentucky fans post videos of them burning UK jerseys because the players had the gall to kneel during the national anthem. One of them is a sheriff from my mom's hometown. I bring as much negative attention as I can to these people and let them know that they are convincing a lot of talented young Black basketball players that the last place they want to come to is Kentucky.

Kentucky fans love to take shots at me on Twitter. More

than a few send me my mug shot. ("This you, bro?") They almost never challenge me in person, although it does happen from time to time. I am in a grocery store once and some guy looks at me real mean. "You're not BBN," he says, which stands for Big Blue Nation.

I want to say, "I scored a thousand points in two years. If that's not BBN, what is?" But I keep shopping.

Another time I am at a gas station and this old white guy—why is it always an old white guy?—comes up and says, "Rex, your life would have been so much better if you thought like the rest of us." He walks away.

I am about to say something obnoxious in reply, but then he turns around and asks, "We gonna beat Bama this weekend?"

● ○ ●

It takes me a while to adjust to living without Zeke. As usual, I haven't given an ounce of thought ahead of time as to what it would be like. I sit on the couch watching a basketball game, and a great play will happen. Instinctively, I shout, "Did you see that?" Nobody hears me but the dog.

During the summer of 2021, CNN offers me a gig as the host of my own interview show for their soon-to-be-launched streaming network, CNN+. The deal is negotiated by my new agent, Jim Ornstein of WME, who is taking great care of me as I try to make this professional transition. Rebecca Kutler is the CNN exec who pushed for me to get this show, and I'm grateful for her belief in me. Before I sign that contract, I am living month to month. Getting my first check only depresses me. I have this deep feeling that I don't deserve it.

The best part of the CNN job is that it means moving to New York City, where I can be close to Zeke. I use the money to buy the condo where I am staying in Lexington from my cousin, and my parents move in. I am all excited about renting an apartment in New York—that is, until they run a credit check on me. I need a guarantor, which is humiliating. I can't even buy a car unless it is with cash.

I know nothing about the TV business. I do a big virtual meeting with the entire company, and the moderator asks me what my "elevator pitch" was to get the show created. I have no idea what an elevator pitch is. (I also hadn't made one. CNN brought the idea to me.) I don't even know what a showrunner is, and I certainly don't realize what a big production it will be. I spend most of that winter rehearsing in a studio, meeting with producers and executives, and developing concepts for the show. As exciting as it is, it is also very unsettling to have so many people depending on me. They need me to be responsive, dependable, and organized, which have never been my strengths. I have a lot of details I need to stay on top of.

For my first episode, I fly to England to do a sit-down with Jason Sudeikis, the producer, writer, and star of the hit show *Ted Lasso*. I've known Jason for a while because he's a huge basketball fan and we have some mutual friends. We do the interview in the bar they use to film the show.

I do another episode with Ben Stiller, who has a hit show

of his own that he is producing for Apple TV+ called *Severance*. Ben and I had connected over Twitter, and once I move to New York, we start meeting for lunch. We talk life, show business, basketball, sports, politics, family, whatever. The whole thing is hilarious and bizarre. I mean, eight years ago I was living in my car, and now I'm having lunch with Ben Stiller. How the fuck did this happen?

The Rex Chapman Show makes its debut in March 2022. One month later, it is toast. CNN has changed ownership, and the new management pulls the plug on the entire venture.

● ○ ●

Brooklyn is a lot different from Lexington, that's for sure. During the first week I live there, I am walking down the street and come upon a food truck. Or at least, I *think* it is a food truck. It is actually a marijuana truck. The woman inside recognizes me and says her cousin is Ed Pinckney, who won an NCAA championship at Villanova and played twelve years in the NBA. I laugh, we high-five, I hand her cash, and she gives me a vape pen. It is that easy.

Marijuana has become a very important component of my mental health. It's mind-boggling to me that it was ever illegal, and it pisses me off that so many people—so many Black people—are still behind bars for marijuana offenses. Marijuana doesn't fix all my problems, but it helps me deal with them better. I typically hit my vape right after my morning coffee. Then I go for a swim and cruise through the workout. I vape once or twice during the afternoon, and again at night. Being on marijuana makes me more social when I am with other people and more at ease when I am alone. I usually use a pen, but once in a while I smoke a joint or eat a gummy. For a disorganized mind like mine, marijuana makes me function better than I ever have as an adult.

Marijuana is not for everybody, and I understand it can be abused. But used properly, it's a lot better—and less addictive—than alcohol, cigarettes, opioids, or many other prescription medicines. Research has shown that marijuana can help heroin and opioid addicts stay off the poison. Yet, medical marijuana is still not legal in a lot of places.

I continue to talk to Kim Peabody, my therapist in Louisville, about once a month. It gives me peace of mind just knowing she is there. I only met Kim in 2014, but it feels like I've known her forever. It's too bad so many people attach a stigma to therapy. When you're struggling, you should seek advice from wherever you can get it. I was desperate enough to try anything, and it worked.

The public's attitude toward therapy seems to be changing, but it's still not acceptable to a lot of people—especially athletes, who are told from a young age that they need to be "mentally tough." We've got to change that. If you're a diabetic, you take insulin, right? If you tear your ACL, you get surgery. Why should it be different for depression? If you're facing mental health challenges and want to feel better and improve your relationships, therapy is a great option. As far as I'm concerned, there's nothing tougher than admitting you have a problem and need some help.

I am disappointed when CNN+ goes under, but by this point there's not much that can rattle me. A few days later, I get a call from Richard Korson, the president of Smartless Media. His company produces the wildly successful *Smartless* podcast hosted by Jason Bateman, Will Arnett, and Sean Hayes. Richard wants me to host a narrative series called *Owned*, where we go in-depth on some of the most famous (and infamous) owners in sports history.

A buddy of mine from Kentucky who's a big political operative asks if I want to run against Rand Paul. The idea of making fun of Rand every day appeals to me, but I tell him no. It's not because I am afraid of losing. I am afraid of *winning*. If that happens, I'll have to have a real job for the first time in my life. Sorry, no interest.

I do, however, say yes in January 2023 to an invitation from the Biden White House to attend a ceremony honoring the Golden State Warriors for their NBA championship. The Biden folks know I am a social media ally, and I am on some email chains with their communications team leading up to the 2022 midterms. The idea that I am invited to that event not by the Warriors but by the White House amuses me to no end. I spend about twenty minutes on the South Lawn hanging with Stephen Curry as he conducts a round of media interviews. Stephen is one of the best players in the world, but when I look at him, I still see a two-year-old kid in the backseat. We're family.

I'm not nearly as rich as I used to be, but that is probably for the best. When I had a lot of money, I found a lot of spectacularly dumb ways to spend it. I still owe the government six figures in back taxes, mostly stemming from my gambling. I am just happy that I can pay my bills each month. At one point, I have to ask Bridget to write an affidavit for me outlining some of my spending habits during the course of our marriage. She agrees but can't resist texting, "There's so much I want to say about this." I am glad she doesn't.

Sleep remains a struggle. I have this weird way of falling asleep that stems from the two years I had to sleep on Josh's couch. It was too short for me, and it was slanted. I had to lie on my side with my legs curled up. Now that's how I sleep all the time. My friends call it my "John McCain position." If I get four hours straight, that is a lot. Sometimes I will sleep for four hours, get up to pee, then get in another one or two. Otherwise, I just lie in bed, wait for the sun to rise, and then start my day. It isn't ideal, but I am used to it.

When I was with the Suns, I used to train with a strength coach named Robin Pound (which is a great name for a strength coach, by the way). His mantra was "Fitness is religion." I didn't know what he meant by that until now. My main exercise is swimming. I swim one hundred laps, which takes me about forty-five minutes. Then I do some push-ups and sit-ups. When I'm working out, I can get out of my head and get my blood pumping. I feel so much better when I'm done, and not just physically. If I don't work out for two or three days, my mental energy diminishes quickly. Working out makes me feel like I've earned my day.

Aside from the marijuana, I take 100 milligrams of Zoloft in the morning, and 100 milligrams of amitriptyline at night to help me sleep. I drink a Coors Light with ice a couple of days a month, but that's it as far as alcohol goes. I'm still the most disorganized person I know. People come to my apartment or look inside my car and they laugh. Everything is scattered. I came to accept long ago that I am missing an organizational component in my brain that most people have. If someone is dependent on Zoloft, you'd think they would order their refills when the bottle gets close to empty. Not me. Sometimes I run out completely and scramble to refill the scrip, which might leave me without the medicine for a couple of days if I'm traveling.

I could say that all these struggles have brought me closer to God. But I'd be lying. I guess I'm more of an agnostic than an atheist. If there is a God, great. If that's not the case, I actually find that to be more reasonable. In the end, I don't think it should matter. We're all here to try to do the best we can and treat people well. We shouldn't need to have God tell us to do those things. I don't know if there is a heaven, but if there is, I hope all my friends and family go there. There do seem to be a lot bad people who are quite certain they're going to heaven. If those people are getting in, I like my chances.

I thought I was depressed in Lexington because I was in Lexington, but I have plenty of bad days in Brooklyn, too. In a weird way, it is healthy for me to realize that I can be miserable anywhere. You can't outrun yourself, no matter how hard you try. In the summer of 2023, I am offered a full-time position as senior personnel advisor and ambassador for the Suns, who have a new owner in Mat Ishbia. The Smartless guys let me out of my contract, which I deeply appreciate. I'm grateful to Mat and his family for allowing me this opportunity. It is gratifying to know that even after all the mistakes I've made, people still respect my basketball experience, knowledge, and relationships. I guess it also means I've treated most people pretty well over the years, even if I didn't love myself all the time. I've always been a pretty one-dimensional guy, so I'm not good at a lot of things. But I can damn sure tell who's a good basketball player. I feel at home in the NBA, and the best part is I get to live near all my kids again.

Believe me, I know how lucky I am to be alive, much less healthy and relatively happy. There's not a day that goes by where I don't feel grateful that I don't have to find a doctor to lie to, or a pharmacist to swindle, or some shady-ass drug dealer to help me get my fix. For so many years, I was resigned to the reality that I would always need that fucking medicine. Now it's been nine years since I took it. I hope I never go back.

●　○　●

I started playing basketball for one reason and one reason only: I liked it. Or rather, I was *good* at it, which made me like it. I wasn't thinking about any reward greater than that. I for sure wasn't thinking about playing in the NBA and getting paid for it, much less millions of dollars.

Whatever came at me between the lines, I could handle it with my eyes closed. I never felt any real pressure on the court. Fuck, I loved it. I was hardwired for that.

All the other shit that came with it, though? I had little to no ability to deal with any of it. And the better I got at basketball, the more the shit piled up. That led me to some pretty dark places.

There's a famous scene in the movie *Good Will Hunting* where Matt Damon is talking with his therapist, played by Robin Williams. The therapist is in a great deal of emotional pain because his wife got cancer and died. Matt, his patient, asks him if he regrets meeting his wife. After all, if he never met and married her, he wouldn't be hurting so much now.

The therapist doesn't hesitate. He has no regrets. He would rather live with the pain than live without the memories of his wife.

That's how I feel about basketball. Being a famous player brought a lot of complications, which were made worse by my short attention span, inclination toward depression, and addictive behaviors. Yet, for all the shit I've been through, for all the mistakes I made, I wouldn't trade one second of my time on the court. I don't even know what I would have done with my life. I never had any other dreams. I knew from a very young age that I was going to take basketball as far as it would take me. I chased that ball as hard as I could, and I loved every minute of it.

There's no feeling like turning the corner, dunking on a seven-footer, and putting him in the basket. There's no elation like the kind I felt when I sank that three-pointer in the playoffs for the Suns, heard the crowd go nuts, and saw my teammates, whom I loved, filled with utter joy. Being an elite player, particularly in Kentucky, probably stunted my intellectual and emotional growth in a lot of ways. I never developed a lot of important life skills because I never had to. I was pushed along in school and rarely held accountable for my fuckups. I made bad decisions in my personal life. I was wholly unprepared for the moment when I would have to retire.

In the end, though, basketball gave me an incredible life. It taught me discipline and teamwork and sacrifice. It taught me how to overcome adversity and take on challenges fearlessly and head-on. It taught me how to be a good teammate. It gave me incredible memories. Best of all, it introduced me to so many people who are amazing and supportive and incredibly impressive. That continues to be the case. The NBA really is one big family. It is full of the best kind of people. I've made more really good friends through basketball than I could possibly count. I can't imagine my life without them.

I've got a lot of regrets, but playing basketball isn't one of them. It shaped who I am, for better and worse. As for all the other shit, well, I remain a work in progress. But at least I'm making progress.

Epilogue

t's the summer of 2023. My dad is now seventy-eight years old. He's had some heart issues and a couple of bouts with COVID, and he got into a bad car wreck a few years ago. He has also taken some bad falls, but that man is tough. So is my mom, who's still got tons of energy despite having knee surgery. My parents live down the street from Josh's mom, and she and my mom have become great friends. It's the sweetest thing ever.

My dad and I are in a good place, all things considered, but it's still hard for us to be around each other sometimes. Unless we're talking about basketball, horse racing, or golf, there's a heaviness in the air. One time I am riding in the car with him and we are talking about Zeke's move to Brooklyn.

"Is he gonna live near the arena?" my dad asks.

"No, he's gonna live in New Jersey and take the bus to work," I snap sarcastically.

After a pause, my dad says softly, "You know I'm just trying to make conversation, don't you?"

I feel like an asshole.

My parents have apologized many times for how they handled the situation with Shawn. I understand they acted the way they did not because of their own prejudices, but because they were concerned about me. They came from a different generation than mine. When they were growing up in Kentucky, they saw some pretty violent acts committed by racists. They were afraid something like that would happen to me. It makes sense, but I still carry some resentment toward how everything went down. My parents and I have had some long talks the last few years, and those have helped.

Unfortunately, things between me and Jenny are still strained. I know I'm at fault, too, and I understand that it was hard growing up in my shadow, but at some point you gotta get over that. Yeah, I got a lot of attention from being good at basketball, but I worked my ass off. Why should I feel bad about that? Jenny and I text each other once in a while, but if we communicate beyond that, there's usually drama. And if there's one thing I need to avoid at this point in my life, it's drama. We're working on making things better between us, although I admit Jenny is working harder than I am.

All that said, I will never, ever forget that Jenny was there for me during my darkest moments. She helped me put my life back together after I was arrested, and she helped me start my new life by letting me live with her in Lexington. I'll admit a part of me is jealous of her, too. Jenny married a Black man named Kio Sanford, who was a really good football player at Kentucky and spent a couple of years in the NFL. They have had their challenges over the years like all couples have, they've been together for more than two decades, and they're doing their best to raise their daughter. I'm sure Jenny knew that marrying a Black guy would upset some people back home, but she absolutely did not give a fuck. She had more courage than I ever did in that regard.

Shawn and I still communicate pretty consistently, usually by text, but the last time we were together was a few years ago when a mutual friend of ours from Kentucky died by suicide. I was happy to see her, but it's always tough for me to be around Shawn. I carry a lot of guilt for the way I treated her. Shawn never got married or had kids, but her niece is like her surrogate daughter, and she's made a good life for herself. She lives in Cincinnati, and when my sister was in town recently, she asked Shawn to meet her for lunch. My mom drove up to join them. I didn't ask for details of what they discussed, but I was glad they had a nice time together.

Bridget and I don't talk a whole lot, either, but we get along fine. We've gotten to the point where we have no problem being around each other if it means being with the kids. Bridget is an incredible mother. When we were arguing and the kids were yelling for food, Bridget was the one who stopped to feed them while I sulked in another part of the house. Bridget is an only child, and she used to worry whether she was capable of parenting more than one kid. She was born to do it, and it was fun to watch her.

When I was living in Kentucky, I started seeing a woman named Whitney Lawson on a regular basis. She makes me laugh and I adore her, but I really don't think I will ever get married again. I wouldn't want to burden any woman by asking her to live with me. That may sound harsh, but it's true. It's hard for *me* to live with me. Sometimes I wish I could take myself in smaller doses, but I guess we're stuck with each other.

● ○ ●

I know that a lot of addicts lose their families and never get them back. Yet, I'm still close to my kids. I guess I must have done something right. I was gone a lot while they were growing up, but I spent a lot of time at home, too, and I went to as many of their activities as I could. I made some mistakes as a dad, but I don't think they ever doubted that I wanted what was best for them.

I couldn't be prouder of my three girls. Caley is an educator who specializes in autism disorders. She's got her own program at the same private school in Phoenix where Bridget teaches. They live together at Bridget's house with Tatum, who is working on my podcasts as a researcher and producer. Tyson finished her degree at the University of Arizona, and in the summer of 2023 she took a job as an assistant program director at a special education transition program for students ages eighteen to twenty-two. I could not be prouder

The girls are each different, which is usually the case with siblings. Caley is funny and silly, but she's real diligent when she needs to be. Tatum and I talk six times a day. Tyson can be a little more standoffish and reserved. We went through periods where she didn't want to hear from me much, which I couldn't blame her for. In 2021, I took Tyson to a Suns game. We had great floor seats and access to a private club. During halftime, we went in there and had some drinks. It was such an awesome time, and I felt such pride over the young woman she was becoming. I told her that night, "I'm sorry for everything I've put you through."

I don't know what made me say it. It just came out. Tyson looked at me and replied, "I really needed to hear you say that."

Zeke had a great first season with the Brooklyn Nets, but he got a rude awakening to life in the NBA when the team fired Steve Nash seven games into the 2022–23 season. Steve was the one who brought Zeke in. He worked the next season with the Nets, and then Frank Vogel, a Kentucky guy, added Zeke to the Suns' staff after Frank got hired to be the head coach. Zeke couldn't resist the opportunity to move back home and be closer to his mom and sister. It looks like he's making a career out of basketball. I'm all for it. It's in his blood, after all.

I love those four people more than I could ever put into words. For them to love me back after everything I've put them through? That's my championship right there.